The Nibelung

English words to Richard Wagner's ring des Nibelungen In the alliterative verse of the original

Alfred Forman

Alpha Editions

This edition published in 2019

ISBN : 9789389525199

Design and Setting By
Alpha Editions
email - alphaedis@gmail.com

As per information held with us this book is in Public Domain.
This book is a reproduction of an important historical work. Alpha Editions uses the best technology to reproduce historical work in the same manner it was first published to preserve its original nature. Any marks or number seen are left intentionally to preserve its true form.

THE
NIBELUNG'S RING

ENGLISH WORDS TO

RICHARD WAGNER'S
RING DES NIBELUNGEN

IN THE ALLITERATIVE VERSE OF THE ORIGINAL

BY

ALFRED FORMAN.

A VERBATIM RE-ISSUE OF THE EDITION OF 1877.
THE ONLY VERSION APPROVED BY THE AUTHOR,
AND THE FIRST TRANSLATION
OF THE WORK INTO ANY LANGUAGE.

LONDON
SCHOTT & CO., 159 REGENT STREET, W.

MAYENCE   PARIS   BRUSSELLS
B. SCHOTT'S SÖHNE P. SCHOTT ET CIE. SCHOTT FRÈRES

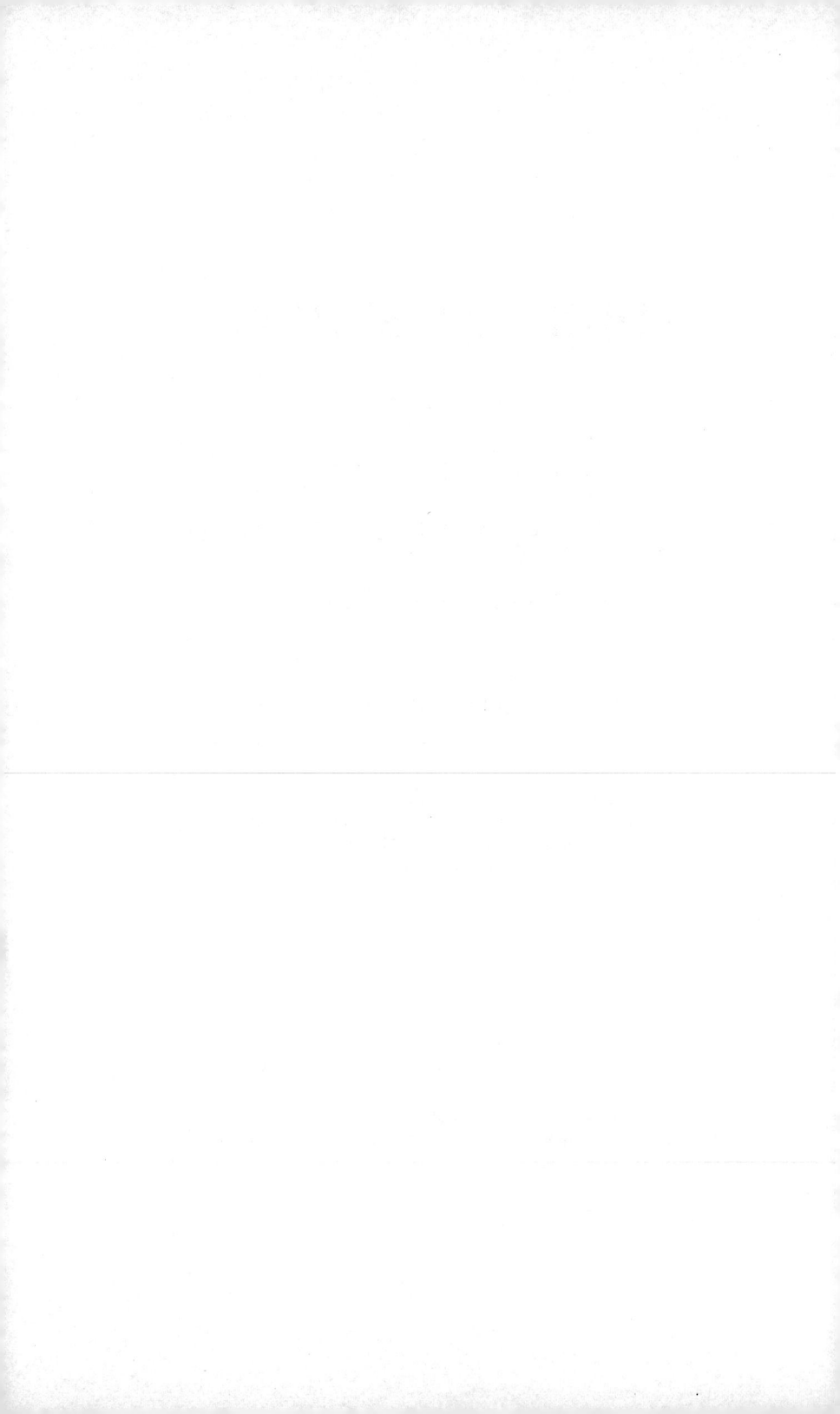

TO RICHARD WAGNER

WITH A PRIVATELY PRINTED COPY OF "THE WALKYRIE."

("*Die Liebe lockte den Lenz.*")

WINTER has waned upon his stormy wing—
the woods are wild with flowers—before my eyes
Spring on the world lies like a lover lies—
the birds have bursts of song for everything—
it seems as if the ceaseless blossoming,
the splendour and the spell can never tire—
for if night comes the moon is like a fire—
and yet my sadness will not let me sing.
Mine is the single sorrow—how shall I
bring to my heart the heart I long to bring?—
My heart so bleeds at my own bitter cry
I taste its blood—as Siegfried, for the ring,
did Fafner's, and a bird, as it goes by,
laughs "Love's enough—'twas Love that lured the
　　Spring!"

Spring, 1873.

FORE-EVENING.

THE RHINEGOLD.

PERSONS.

WOTAN,
DONNER, } Gods.
FROH,
LOGE,

FASOLT, } Giants.
FAFNER,

ALBERICH, } Nibelungs.
MIME,

FRICKA,
FREIA, } Goddesses.
ERDA,

WOGLINDE,
WELLGUNDE, } Rhine-Daughters.
FLOSSHILDE,

Nibelungs.

THE RHINEGOLD.

AT THE BOTTOM OF THE RHINE.

(Greenish twilight—lighter upwards, darker downwards. The upper part is filled with waves of moving water that stream restlessly from right to left. Towards the bottom the water is dissolved into a gradually finer and finer wet mist, so that the space of a man's height from the ground seems to be quite free from water, which flows like a train of clouds over the dark depth. Everywhere rugged ridges of rock rise from the bottom, and form the boundary of the scene. The whole floor is broken into a wilderness of jagged masses, so that it is nowhere perfectly level, and indicates in every direction deeper passages stretching into thickest darkness.

In the middle of the scene, round a ridge which, with its slender point, reaches up into the thicker and lighter water, one of the Rhine-Daughters swims in graceful movement.)

WOGLINDE.

Weia ! Waga !
Waver, thou water !
Crowd to the cradle !
Wagalaweia !
Wallala weiala weia !

WELLGUNDE'S
(voice from above).
Watchest thou, Woglind', alone ?

WOGLINDE.
Till Wellgund' is with me below.

WELLGUNDE
(dives down from the flood to the ridge).
Is wakeful thy watch ?
(She tries to catch Woglinde.)

WOGLINDE
(swims out of her reach).
Safe from thee so.
(They incite and seek playfully to catch each other).

FLOSSHILDE'S
(voice from above).

Heiala weia!
Wisdomless sisters!

WELLGUNDE.

Flosshilde, swim!
Woglinde flies;
help me her flowing to hinder!

FLOSSHILDE
(dives down and swims between them as they play).

The sleeping gold
slightly you guard;
better beset
the slumberer's bed,
or grief will bring us your game!

(*With merry cries they swim away from each other; Flosshilde tries to catch first one and then the other; they slip from her, and then together give chase to Flosshilde; so, laughing and playing, they dart like fish from ridge to ridge.*
Meanwhile Alberich has come out of a dark chasm from below, and climbs up a ridge. Still surrounded by the darkness, he stops and observes with growing pleasure the games of the water-maidens.)

ALBERICH.

Hi hi! you Nodders!
How neat I find you!
Neighbourly folk!
From Nibelheim's night
I soon will be near,
if made I seem to your mind.

(*The maidens, on hearing Alberich's voice, stop their play.*)

WOGLINDE.

Hi! what is here?

WELLGUNDE.

It whispered and gleamed.

FLOSSHILDE.

Watch who gazes this way.
(*They dive deeper down, and perceive the Nibelung.*)

WOGLINDE and WELLGUNDE.
Fie ! what frightfulness !

FLOSSHILDE
(swimming swiftly up).
Guard the gold !
Father said
that such was the foe.

(*The two others follow her, and all three gather quickly round the middle ridge.*)

ALBERICH.
You there aloft !

THE THREE.
What leads thee below ?

ALBERICH.
Spoil I your sport,
if here you hold me in spell ?
Dive to me deeper ;
with you to dance
and dabble the Nibelung yearns !

WELLGUNDE.
Our play will he join in ?

WOGLINDE.
Passed he a joke ?

ALBERICH.
How fast and sweetly
you flash and swim !
The waist of one
I would soon undauntedly wind,
slid she dreadlessly down !

FLOSSHILDE.
Now laugh I at fear ;
the foe is in love.
(*They laugh*).

WELLGUNDE.
And look how he longs!

WOGLINDE.
Now shall we near him?

She lets herself down to the point of the peak, whose foot Alberich has reached.)

ALBERICH.
She lets herself low.

WOGLINDE.
Now come to me close!

ALBERICH
(climbs with imp-like agility, but stopping often on the way, towards the point of the peak).

Sleek as slime
the slope of the slate is!
I slant and slide!
With foot and with fist
I no safety can find
on the slippery slobber!
(He sneezes.)
A sniff of wet
has set me sneezing;
the cursed snivel!
(He has reached the neighbourhood of Woglinde.)

WOGLINDE
(laughing).
With winning cough
my wooer comes!

ALBERICH.
My choice thou wert,
thou womanly child!
(He tries to embrace her.)

WOGLINDE
(winding out of his way).
Here, if thy bent
I heed, it must be!
She has reached another ridge. The sisters laugh.)

The Rhinegold.

ALBERICH
(scratches his head).
O grief! thou art gone!
Come though again!
Large for me
is the length of thy leap.

WOGLINDE
(springs to a third ridge lower down).
Sink to my side,
and fast thou shalt seize me!

ALBERICH
(climbs quickly down).
Below it is better!

WOGLINDE
darts quickly upwards to a high side-ridge).
Aloft I must bring thee!
(All the maidens laugh.)

ALBERICH.
How follow and catch I
the crafty fish?
Fly not so falsely!
(He attempts to climb hastily after her.)

WELLGUNDE
(has sunk down to a lower reef on the other side).
Heia! thou sweetheart!
Hear what I say!

ALBERICH
(turning round).
Wantest thou me?

WELLGUNDE.
I mean to thee well;
this way turn thyself,
try not for Woglind'!

ALBERICH
(climbs quickly over the bottom to Wellgunde).
More fair I find thee
than her I followed,

who shines less sweetly
and slips aside.—
But glide more down,
if good thou wilt do me!

WELLGUNDE
(*sinking down still lower towards him*).
And now am I near?

ALBERICH.
Not yet enough!
Thy slender arms
O set me within;
feel in thy neck
how my fingers shall frolic;
in burying warmth
shall bear me the wave of thy bosom.

WELLGUNDE.
Art thou in love,
and aim'st at delight?
If so, thy sweetness
I first must see!—
Fie! how humpy
and hidden in hair!
Black with brimstone
and hardened with burns!
Seek for a lover
liker thyself!

ALBERICH
(*tries to hold her by force*).
Unfit though I'm found
I'll fetter thee safe!

WELLGUNDE
(*darting quickly up to the middle peak*).
Quite safe, or forth I shall swim!
(*All three laugh.*)

ALBERICH
out of temper, scolding after her).
Fitful child!
Chafing and frosty fish!

Seem I not sightly,
pretty and playful,
smiling and smooth?
Eels I leave thee for lovers,
if at my skin thou can scold!

FLOSSHILDE.

What say'st thou, dwarf?
So soon upset?
But two thou hast asked
try for the other—
with healing hope
let her allay thy harm!

ALBERICH.

Soothing words
to-wards me are sung.—
How well in the end
that you all are not one!
To one of a number I'm welcome;
though none of one were to want me!—
Let me believe thee,
and draw thee below!

FLOSSHILDE

(dives down to Alberich)

What silly fancy,
foolish sisters,
fails to see he is fair?

ALBERICH

(quickly approaching her).

Both dull and hateful
here I may deem them,
since I thy sweetness behold.

FLOSSHILDE

(flatteringly).

O sound with length
thy lovely song;
my sense it loftily lures!

ALBERICH
(touching her trustfully).
My heart shakes
and shrivels to hear
showered so pointed a praise.

FLOSSHILDE
(gently repulsing him).
Thy charm besets me
and cheers my sight;
in thy leaping laughter
my heart delights!
(She draws him tenderly to her).
Sorrowless man!

ALBERICH
Sweetest of maids!

FLOSSHILDE.
Art thou my own?

ALBERICH.
All and for ever!

FLOSSHILDE
(holding him quite in her arms).
I am stabbed with thy stare,
with thy beard I am stuck;
O let me not loose from the bliss!
In the hold of thy fixed
and furrowing hair
be Flosshild' floated to heaven!
At thy shape like a toad,
to the shriek of thy tongue,
O let me in answerless spell,
look and hearken alone!
*Woglinde and Wellgunde have dived down close to them and now break
out into ringing laughter.)*

ALBERICH
(starting in alarm out of Flosshilde's arms).
Make you laughter at me?

The Rhinegold.

FLOSSHILDE
(breaking suddenly from him).

We send it as last of the song.
(She darts upwards with her sisters and joins in their laughter.)

ALBERICH
(with shrieking voice).

Woe! Ah, Woe!
O grief! O grief!
The third to my trust
is treacherous too?—
You giggling, gliding
gang of unmannerly maidens!
Feel you no touch,
you truthless Nodders, of faith?

THE THREE RHINE-DAUGHTERS.

Wallala! Lalaleia! Lalei!
Heia! Heia! Haha!
Lower thy loudness!
Bluster no longer!
Learn the bent of our bidding!
What made thee faintly
free in the midst
the maid who fixed thy mind?
True finds us
and fit for trust
the wooer who winds us tight.
Freshen thy hope,
and hark to no fear;
in the flood we hardly shall flee.

*They swim away from each other, hither and thither, now higher an
now lower, to provoke Alberich to chase them.)*

ALBERICH.

How in my body
blistering heat
upheaves the blood!
Lust and hate
with heedless longing
harrow my heart up!

Laugh and lie as you will,
wide alight is my want
till ease from one of you end it!

(*With desperate efforts he begins to pursue them, with fearful nimbleness he climbs ridge after ridge, springs from one to the other, and tries to seize now this maiden, now that, who always escape from him with mocking laughter; he stumbles, falls into the depth below, and then climbs hastily up again—till at last he loses all patience; breathless, and foaming with rage, he stops, and stretches his clenched fist up towards the maidens.*)

ALBERICH
(*almost beside himself*).
This fist on one to fix!

(*He remains looking upwards in speechless rage till his attention is suddenly caught and held by the following spectacle:
Through the flood from above a gradually brighter light has penetrated, which now, at a high spot in the middle peak, kindles into a blinding golden glare; a magical yellow light breaks thence through the water.*)

WOGLINDE.
Look, sisters!
The wakener's laugh is below.

WELLGUNDE.
Through the grassy gloom
the slumberer sweetly it greets.

FLOSSHILDE.
Now kisses its eye
and calls it to open;
lo, it smiles
in the smiting light;
through the startled flood
flows the stream of its star.

THE THREE
(*gracefully swimming round the peak together*)
Heiayaheia!
Heiayaheia!
Wallalallalala leiayahei!
Rhinegold!
Rhinegold!
Burning delight,

how bright is thy lordly laugh !
  Holy and red
the river behold in thy rise !
  Heiayahei !
  Heiayaheia !
  Waken, friend,
  fully wake !
  Gladdening games
  around thee we guide ;
  flames are aflow,
  floods are on fire ;
  with sound and with song,
  with dives and with dances,
we bathe in the depth of thy bed.
  Rhinegold !
  Rhinegold !
  Heiayaheia !
  Wallalaleia yahei !

ALBERICH
(*whose look is strongly attracted by the light, and remains fixed on the gold*).
  What's that, you gliders,
  that there so gleams and glows ?

THE THREE MAIDENS
(*by turns*).
  Where is the wonderer's home,
who of Rhinegold never has heard ?—
    He guessed not aught
    of the golden eye
  that wakes and wanes again ?
    Of the darting star
    that stands in the deep
  and lights the dark with a look ?—
    See how gladly
    we swim in its glances !
    Bathe with us
    in the beam thy body,
  and fear no further its blaze !
      (*They laugh.*)

ALBERICH.
Is the gold but good
for your landless games?
I lean to it little!

WOGLINDE.
To the matchless toy
more he would take,
were he told of its wonder!

WELLGUNDE.
The world's wealth
is by him to be won,
who has from the Rhinegold
hammered the ring
that helps him to measureless might.

FLOSSHILDE.
Father it was
who warned us, fast
and whole to guard him
the gleaming hoard
that no foe from the flood might seize it;
so check your chattering song!

WELLGUNDE.
What brings, besetting
sister, thy blame?
Hast thou not learned
who alone,
that lives, to forge it is fit?

WOGLINDE.
Who from delight
of love withholds,
who for its might
has heed no more,
alone he reaches the wonder
that rounds the gold to a ring.

WELLGUNDE.

No dread behoves it
to daunt us here;
for life without love is unknown of;
none with its pastime will part.

WOGLINDE.

And hardest the deed
to the hankering dwarf;
with fire of love
he looks to be faint!

FLOSSHILDE.

I fear him not
as I found him now;
with his love he soon
would have set me alight.

WELLGUNDE.

Like a brimstone brand
in the waves he burned;
with heat of love
he hissed aloud.

THE THREE.
(together).

Wallalalleia! Lahei!
Wildering lover,
wilt thou not laugh?
In the swaying gold
how softly thou gleam'st!
Why sound we our laughter alone?
(They laugh.)

ALBERICH

with his eyes fixed on the gold has listened to the hurried chatter of the sisters).

The world's wealth
by the might of thy means I may win—

and forced I not love,
yet delight at the least I might filch!
(Fearfully loud.)
Laugh as you like!
The Nibelung nears you at last!

(With rage he leaps to the middle peak and climbs with terrible speed towards its top. The maidens dart asunder with cries and swim upwards in different directions.)

THE THREE RHINE-DAUGHTERS.

Heia! Heia! Heiahahei!
See to yourselves!
The dwarf is unsafe!
How the water spits
where he has sprung;
with love his wits he has lost!

(They laugh in maddest merriment.)

ALBERICH
(at the top of the peak stretching his hand towards the gold.)

Dream you no dread?
Then smother the dark
your drivelling smiles!
Your light let I begone;
the gold I clutch from the rock
and clench to the greatening ring;
for lo! how I curse
love, be witness the water!

(He seizes, with fearful force, the gold from the ridge, and plunges headlong with it into the depth where he swiftly disappears. Thick night breaks suddenly in on all sides. The maidens dart straight after the the thief down into the depth.)

THE RHINE-DAUGHTERS
(screaming).

Grasp the stealer!
Stop the gold!
Help! Help!
Woe! Woe!

(The flood falls with them down towards the bottom; from the lowest depth is heard Alberich's yelling laughter. The ridges disappear in thickest darkness; the whole scene, from top to bottom, is filled with black waves of water that for some time still seem to sink downwards.)

The Rhinegold.

(*By degrees the waves change into clouds which become gradually clearer, and when at last they have quite disappeared, as it were in fine mist,*

AN OPEN DISTRICT ON MOUNTAIN-HEIGHTS

becomes visible, at first still dim with night. The breaking day lightens with growing brightness a castle with shining battlements that stands upon a point of rock in the background; between this castle-crowned rock and the foreground of the scene lies, as is to be supposed, a deep valley, with the Rhine flowing through it. At the side on flowery ground lies Wotan with Fricka beside him; both are asleep.)

FRICKA
(*awakes, her eye falls on the castle; she is surprised and alarmed*).

Wotan ! Husband ! Awaken !

WOTAN
(*lightly in his dream*)

The happy hall of delight
is locked amid gate and guard ;
   manhood's worship,
   measureless might,
mount to unfinishing fame !

FRICKA
(*shakes him*).

  Up from the dreadless
  drift of thy dreams !
Awake, and weigh what thou doest !

WOTAN
(*awakes, and raises himself a little; his eye is immediately caught by sight of the castle*).

Behold the unwithering work !
  With heeding towers
  the height is tipped ;
  broadly stands
  the stately abode !
  As I drew it in dream—
  as it was in my will—
  safe and fair
  finds it my sight,—
holy, sheltering home !

FRICKA.

So meet thou deemest
what most is my dread?
Thy welcomed walls
for Freia beware of.
Waken and be not unmindful
to what a meed thou art bound!
    The work is ended
    and owed for as well;
forgettest thou what thou must give?

WOTAN.

Forgotten not is the guerdon
they named who worked at the walls;
    the unbending team
    by bargain I tamed,
    that here the lordly
    hall might be lifted;
they piled it—thanks befall them;—
for the pay fret not thy thought.

FRICKA.

O light unmerciful laughter!
Loveless masterly mischief!
Had I but heard of your freak,
its fraud would wholly have failed;
    but boldly you worked it
    abroad from the women,—
where safe from sight you were left
alone with the giants to juggle.
    So without shame
    or shyness you sold them
Freia, my flowering sister,—
and deemed it sweetly was done.—
    What to you men
    for worship is meet,
when your minds are on might?

WOTAN.

Was Wotan's want

The Rhinegold.

from Fricka so far,
who sought for the fastness herself?

FRICKA.

Of my husband's truth was my heed;
I tried, in soundless sorrow,
how to find him the fetters
fittest to hold him at home;
    lordly abode
    and blissful living
lightly with bitless reins
should bind thee to lingering rest;
thy bent for the building leaned
on fence and fight alone;
    worship and might
    thou mean'st it to widen;
that steadier storm may betide thee
thou turn'st to its towering strength.

WOTAN
(smiling).

Wert thou to grasp me
in guard like a woman,
thou yet must yield to my godhood
    that, in the bulwarks
    irked and bounded,
the world it outwards should win.
    Freedom and freshness
    he loves who lives;
I part not lightly with pastime.

FRICKA.

    Hard, unmoved
    and harassing man!
    For might and lordship's
    meaningless lure,
thou scatter'st in loudness of scorn
love and a woman's worth!

WOTAN
(earnestly).

To earn a wife in thee was it
    my other eye
went into pledge when I wooed;
how blindly passed is thy blame!
    Women I worship
    too far for thy wish;
    and Freia, the sweet'ner,
    sell I not forth;
I meant not such in my mind.

FRICKA.

Then shield her to-day;
    in shelterless dread
hither she dashes for help!

FREIA
(entering hurriedly).

Ward me, sister!
See to me, Wotan!
For Fasolt roars,
    from the ridge of his fastness,
his fist is ready to fetch me.

WOTAN.

Let him howl!—
Beheld'st thou not Loge?

FRICKA.

How besettingly try'st thou
    his slyness with trust!
Though harm we have stood at his hands,
he clouds thee still with his cunning.

WOTAN.

Where manly mood counts
I call none of my neighbours;
    but to find in hate
    of foes a friendship,
cunning only and craft,

with Loge to lead them, can aid.
He, whom I hearkened to, swore
to find a safety for Freia;
on him my hope I have set.

FRICKA.

And he leaves thee alone.—
    Here stride instead
    the giants in storm;
where slinks thy slippery stay?

FREIA.

What hinders my brothers
from help they should bring me,
when of Wotan's my weakness is bare?
    Behold me, Donner!
    Hither! Hither!
Haste to Freia, my Froh!

FRICKA.

In the heartless bargain who bound thee,
they hide their best from thee here.

(*Fasolt and Fafner enter, both of giants' stature, and armed with strong stakes.*)

FASOLT.

    Soft sleep
    sealed thy sight;
    we set meanwhile
unslumb'ringly the walls.
    Nameless toil
    tired us not;
    strength of stone
    on high we stowed;
    deep in towers,
    tight with doors,
    holds and seals
the slender house its hall.
    Well stands
    what we steepened,

decked with light
of laughing dawn ;—
pass the gate,
and give the pay!

WOTAN.

Name, neighbours, your meed;
what like you most to light on?

FASOLT.

The rate we mean
already is marked;
I find thy memory faint.
Freia, the holder—
Holda, the freer—
we have thy word—
her win we for home.

WOTAN.

Sick is thy brain
with bargain and sale?
Think on fitter thanks;
Freia I sell not so.

FASOLT
(*for a moment speechless with rage and surprise*).
What hear I? Ha!
Brood'st thou on harm,
on hurt to the bond?
On thy spear written
read'st thou as sport
the runes that bound the bargain?

FAFNER
(*sneering*).
My trusty brother!
Tells the blockhead a trap?

FASOLT.

Light-son, lightly
made and minded,
hark with timely heed—

and truthful be to bonds !
    All thou art
abides but under a bargain ;
    in measured mood
wisely weighed was thy might.
       Thou warier wert
       than we in thy wits,
       wielded'st our freedom
       to friendly ways ;
curses await thy wisdom,
far I keep from thy friendship,
       find I thee aught
       but open and fair
when faith to thy bargains is bid !
    A senseless giant
    so has said ;
though wiser, see it his way !

        WOTAN.

How slily thou say'st we meant
what passed at playtime among us !
    The flowery goddess,
       gleaming and fleet,
would blind you both with a glance !

        FASOLT.

   Must thou mock ?
   Ha ! is it meet ?—
You who for fairness rule,
young unfaltering race,
    like fools you strive
    for a fastness of stone,
put for house and hall
worth of woman in pledge !
    We sorely hasten
and sweat with hardening hand,
    till won is a woman
    with sweetening ways
    beside us to wait ;—
and upset wilt thou the sale ?

FAFNER.

Balk thy worthless babble!
For wealth woo we no bit!
    Faintly help us
    Freia's fetters;
    yet much grows
if once from the gods we can get her.
    Golden apples
there are in her gleaming garden;
    none but her
has the knowledge to nurse them;
    the kindly fruit
    kindles her fellows
    to youth that bears
    unyellowing blossom;
    far at once
    they wane from their flower,
    weak and low
    will they be left,
when Freia feeds them no longer;
from their faces let her be led!

WOTAN
(to himself).

Loge saunters long!

FASOLT.

Make swiftly thy mind!

WOTAN.

Point to lighter pay!

FASOLT.

No lower; Freia alone!

FAFNER.

Thou there, follow forth!
(They press towards Freia.)

FREIA
(fleeing).

Help! Help! they will have me!
(Donner and Froh hurry in.)

The Rhinegold.

FROH
(taking Freia in his arms).
To me, Freia !—
Meddle no further !
Froh saves his sister.

DONNER
(placing himself before the giants).
Fasolt and Fafner
have halted before
at my hammer's hearty fall !

FAFNER.
What wilt thou threat ?

FASOLT.
Who thrusts this way ?
Fight fits us not now ;
we need what fairly we named.

DONNER
(swinging his hammer).
I judged oft
what giants are owed ;
rested no day
in wretches' debt ;
behold ! your guerdon here
I give you in worthy weight !

WOTAN
(stretching out his spear between the opponents).
Hold, thou haster !
Force is unfit !
I shield the words
on my weapon's shaft ;
beware for thy hammer's hilt !

FREIA.
Sorrow ! Sorrow !
Wotan forsakes me !

FRICKA.
As hitherto hard
find I thy heart?

WOTAN
(*turns away and sees Loge coming*).
Loge at last!—
Com'st thou so soon
to see me unclasped
from the cursed bond of thy bargain?

LOGE
(*has come in from the background, out of the valley*).
Why? from what bargain
where I have bound thee?
The one that the giants
joined thee wisely to work?—
For heights and for hollows
hankers my heart;
house and hearth
not a day I hold;
Donner and Froh
are fonder of roof and room;
when they will woo,
a house wait they to have;
a stately hall,
a standing home,
were what stirred Wotan's wish.—
House and hall—
wall and wing—
the laughing abode—
at last is broadly built;
the soaring towers
I tested myself;
if all was hard
I asked with heed;
Fasolt and Fafner
I found were fair;
not a stone flinched where it stood.
No sloven was I
like some I see;
he lies who says I was lame!

WOTAN.

So slily
slipp'st thou aside?
How thou betray'st me
take the whole of thy heed!
Among us all
not another moved
even with me
to up-aid thee into our midst.—
Now spur thy wits and speak!
When first as worth of their walls
the workmen fixed upon Freia,
thou saw'st I would
no sooner be won
than on thy oath I had put thee
to loosen the lordly pledge.

LOGE.

With lasting heed
to look for hints
of how we might loose her—
such wholly I swore;
but now to find thee
what never fits—
what needs must fail,
a bond could nowhere have bound me!

FRICKA
(to Wotan).

Wronged I lately
the lingering rogue?

FROH.

Thou art known as Loge,
but liar I name thee!

DONNER.

Thou cursed fire,
I'll crush thee flat!

LOGE.
Their blame to screen
scold me the babies.
Donner and Froh prepare to attack him.)

WOTAN
(*forbidding them*).
In freedom leave me my friend,
and scorn not Loge's skill;
richer worth
in his words is read
when counted well as they come.

FAFNER.
Push the counting!
Quickly pay!

FASOLT.
Much palters the meed!

WOTAN
(*to Loge*).
Await, harasser!
Hark to me well!
What was it that held thee away?

LOGE.
Threats are what Loge
learns of thanks!
In heed for thy strait
I hied like a storm,
I drifted and drove
through the width of the world,
to find a ransom for Freia—
fit for the giants and fair.
I looked soundly,
but see that at last
in the wheeling world
lies not the wealth,
that can weigh in mind of a man
for woman's wonder and worth.
(*All fall into surprise and confusion.*)

Where life is to be lit on,
in water, earth, and wind,
    I asked always,
    sought without end,
    where forces beset,
    and seeds are unfettered,
    what has in mind
    of man more weight
than woman's wonder and worth?
But where life is to be lit on,
    to scorn I was laughed
    for my questioning skill;
in water, earth, and wind,
    nothing will loose
    from woman and love.—
    But one I learned of
at last who had warred on love;
    for gleaming gold
from woman he widely goes.
The Rhine's bemoaning children
chattered to me their wrong;
    the Nibelung,
    Night-Alberich,
    bade them in vain
bend to his voice in their bath;
    the Rhinegold then
and there from the river he rent;
    he holds its glance
    his holiest good,
and greater than woman's worth.
    For the flickering toy,
    so torn from the flood,
they sounded their tale of sorrow;
    thy side, Wotan,
    soon they will seek;
thou wilt rightly see to the robber,
    its wealth again
    wilt give the water,
and sink it away into safety.—
    Such are the tidings

I said I would take thee;—
so Loge told them no lie.

WOTAN.

Wanton thou art,
or else bewildered!
Myself see'st thou in need;
what help is now in my hands?

FASOLT
(who has carefully listened, to Fafner).

The gold from the dwarf should be guarded,
much wrong he has done us already;
but slily always slipped he
out of reach of our wrath.

FAFNER.

Harm anew
the Niblung will hatch us,
now that the gold he has got.—
Swiftly, Loge,
say without lies,
what good is known of the gold,
that the Niblung sought it so?

LOGE.

A lump was it
below the water,
children to laughter it charmed:
but when to a ring
it rightly is welded,
it helps to highest might
and wins its master the world.

WOTAN.

Of the Rhinegold were
already whispers;
runes of booty
abide in its ruddy blaze.
Might and riches
would make without measure a ring.

FRICKA.

Would not as well
the golden wealth
be worn with its gleam
by women for shining show?

LOGE.

A wite might force
her husband to faith,
held she in hand
the sparkling heaps
that spring from hurrying hammers
raised at the spell of the ring.

FRICKA.

My husband will get
the gold to him here?

WOTAN.

The hoop to have with me
hold I wholly for wisdom.—
But hark, Loge,
how shall I learn
the means that let it be made?

LOGE.

By spell of runes
is wrought the speeding ring;
none has known it;
yet each can wield its aid,
who weans from love his life.

(*Wotan turns away with disgust.*)

Thy loss were ill,
and late moreover;
Alberich lingered not off;
swiftly he severed
the wonder's seal;
and rightly welded the ring.

DONNER.
Ill would dwell
for us all in the dwarf,
if long we the ring were to leave him.

WOTAN.
The robber must lose it!

FROH.
Lightly lo
without curse of love will it come.

LOGE
Gladly as laughter,
without pain in a game of play!

WOTAN.
But hear me, how?

LOGE.
By theft!
What a thief stole
thou steal'st from the thief;
could gain be more thankfully got?
But with artful foil
fences Alberich;
brisk and sly
be in the business,
call'st thou the robber to claim,
that the river's maidens
their ruddy mate,
the gold, back may be given;
for so as I said they will beg.

WOTAN.
The river's maidens?
What mean they to me

FRICKA.
Of the trickling breed
bring me no tidings;

for many men,
with loss to me
already they reft from the light.

(*Wotan stands in silent conflict with himself; the other gods, in speechless anxiety, fix their eyes on him. Meanwhile, Fafner, aside, has consulted with Fasolt.*)

FAFNER.

Mark that more than Freia
fits us the glittering gold;
and endless youth is as good,
though by spell of gold it be got.

(*They come near again.*)

Hear, Wotan,
a word while we halt!
Live with Freia in freedom;
lighter rate
find I of ransom;
for greedless giants enough
is the Nibelung's ready gold.

WOTAN.

Wander your wits?
What is not my wealth,
to askers like you can I yield?

FAFNER.

Long work
uplifted thy walls;
light were it,
by warier ways
than our hatred happened to know,
to fetter the Niblung fast.

WOTAN.

For such—now
to seize on the Niblung?
For such—fight with the foe?
Unabashed
and overbearing
I think you under my thanks!

FASOLT
(suddenly seizes Freia and takes her with Fafner aside).
To me, Maid!
For home we make!
In pledge rest for our toil,
till thy ransom is paid.

(Freia shrieks; all the gods are in the greatest alarm.)
FAFNER.
Fast along
let her be led!
Till evening—hear me out—
her we pin as a pledge;
we back will bring her;
but if it be
that we find ready no ransom
of Rhinegold fit and red—

FASOLT.
We wrangle no further,
Freia, as forfeit,
for ever follows us off!

FREIA.
Sister! Brother!
Save me, both!

(The giants hurriedly drag her off: the troubled gods hear her cries of distress die away in the distance.)
FROH.
Up, to her aid!

DONNER.
Bar me not any!
(They question Wotan with their looks.)
LOGE
(looking after the giants).
Over stump and stone they heave
hence like a storm;
through the river's forded reach
fiercely they flounder;

The Rhinegold.

Freia seems
far from sweetly
to sit the shape of their shoulders!
Heia! Hei!
How bluster the blockheads along!
In the land hang not their heels;
nought but Riesenheim's bound
now will bring them to rest!

(*He turns to the gods.*)
Why left is Wotan so wild?
How goes the luck of the gods?

(*A pale mist with increasing thickness fills the stage; in it the gods soon put on a look of growing whiteness and age; all stand looking with trouble and expectation at Wotan, who fixes his eyes on the ground in thought.*)

LOGE.

Mocks me a dream,
or drowns me a mist?
How sick and sad
you suddenly seem!
In your cheeks the light is checked;
the cheer of your eyes is at end!—
Up, my Froh,
yet early it is!—
In thy hand, Donner,
what deadens the hammer?—
Why grieved is Fricka?
Greets she so faintly
the grayness Wotan has got,
to warn him all must be old?

FRICKA.

Sorrow! Sorrow!
Why are we so?

DONNER.

My hand is stayed.

FROH.

My heart is still.

LOGE.
Behold it! Hark what has happened!
    On Freia's fruit
I doubt if you feasted to-day;
    the golden apples
    out of her garden
have yielded you dower of youth,
ate you them every day.
    The garden's feeder
    in forfeit is guarded;
    on the branches frets
    and browns the fruit—
and rots right to its fall.—
    My need is milder;
    to me never
    Freia has given
gladly the fostering food;
    for barely half
so whole I was bred as you here!
    But your welfare you fixed
    on the work of the fruit,
and well were the giants ware;
    a trap they laid
    to tangle your life,
which look how to uphold!
    Without the apples,
    old and hoar—
    hoarse and helpless—
worth not a dread to the world,
the dying gods must grow.

FRICKA.
Wotan! Husband!
    Where is thy hope?
    Own that thy laughing
    lightness has ended
in wrong and wreck for all!

WOTAN
(starting up with sudden decision).
Up, Loge!

The Rhinegold.

And let us be off!
To Nibelheim now together!
At hazards I'll have the gold.

LOGE.

The Rhine-maidens
moan for their rights—
and may they not hope for thy hearing?

WOTAN
(impetuously).

Tush, thou talker!
Freia—befriending
Freia rests for her ransom.

LOGE.

Fast as thou like
let it befall;
right below
nimbly I lead through the Rhine.

WOTAN.

Not through the Rhine!

LOGE.

Then come to the brim
of the brimstone cleft,
and slip inside with me so!

(*He goes first and disappears sideways in a cleft, out of which immediately flows a sulphurous mist.*)

WOTAN.

You others, halt
till evening here;
for faded youth
the fresh'ner is yet to be found!

(*He goes down after Loge into the cleft; the mist that rises out of it spreads itself over the whole scene and quickly fills it with a thick cloud. Already those who stay behind have become invisible.*)

DONNER.

Farewell, Wotan!

FROH.

Good luck! Good luck!

FRICKA.

O soon again
be safe at my side!

(*The mist darkens till it becomes a perfectly black cloud, which moves from below upwards: this changes itself into a firm dark chasm of rock, that still moves in an upward direction, so that it seems as if the stage were sinking deeper and deeper into the earth.*
At length from different directions in the distance dawns a dusky red light: a vast far-stretching

SUBTERRANEAN CAVERN.

becomes visible, which on all sides seems to issue in narrow passages. Alberich drags the shrieking Mime by the ear out of a side-cleft.)

ALBERICH.

Hihi! Hihi!
To me! To me!
Try not thy tricks!
Lustily now
look to be lashed,
find I not finished
fitly and well
at once the work that I fixed!

MIME

(*howling*).

Oho! Oho!
Oh! Oh!
Let me alone!
Ready it lies!
Rightfully wrought,
with sores and sweat
not to be named;
off with thy nail from my ear!

ALBERICH

(*loosing him*).

Why saunter so long
to let me see?

MIME.

It struck me something
might still beseem it.

ALBERICH.

What stays to be settled?

MIME
(*confused*).

This . . . and that . . .

ALBERICH.

What "that and this"?
Hither the whole!

(*He seeks to seize him again by the ear: in fright Mime lets fall a piece of metal-work that he held convulsively in his hands. Alberich instantly picks it up and examines it with care.*)

So thou rogue!
See it is ready,
and finished as most
fits to my mind!
So fancied the sot
slily to foil me,
and take the masterly
toy that he made
only by help
of a hint of my own?
Thoughtless and hasty thief!

(*He puts the work as "Tarn-helm" on his head.*)

The helm sets to my head;
see, if the wonder will work?
—"Night and darkness,
know me none!"

(*His figure disappears; in his place a pillar of cloud is seen.*)

See'st thou me, brother?

MIME
(*looks wonderingly about*).

What bars thee? I see thee no bit.

ALBERICH'S
(*voice*).
Then feel me instead,
thou standing fool!
Be weaned from thy stealthy whims!
Mime screams and writhes under the strokes of a whip whose fall is heard, without the whip itself being visible.)

ALBERICH'S
(*voice, laughing*).
Thanks, thou thinker,
for wise and thorough work.—
Hoho! Hoho!
Nibelungs all,
kneel now to Alberich!
Everywhere waits he
and watches his workmen;
rest and room
are you bereft of;
now you must serve him
though not in your sight;
when he seems to be far—
he fully besets you;
under him all are for ever!
Hoho! Hoho!
Lo he is near,
the Nibelungs' lord!

(*The pillar of cloud disappears towards the background; Alberich's angry scolding is heard gradually farther and farther off; from the lower clefts he is answered by howls and cries, the sound of which by degrees dies out in the further distance. Mime for pain has fallen to the ground; his whimpering and groaning are heard by Wotan and Loge who descend by a cleft from above.*)

LOGE.
Nibelheim here;
through hindering film
what a sputter of fiery sparkles!

WOTAN.
Who groans so loud;
what lies on the ground?

LOGE
(bends down to Mime).
Who is the whimperer here?

MIME.
Oho! Oho!
Oh! Oh!

LOGE.
Hi, Mime! merry dwarf!
What frets and forces thee down?

MIME.
Mind not the matter!

LOGE.
Such is my meaning;
and more, behold;
help I have for thee, Mime!

MIME
(raising himself a little).
Who sides with me?
I serve the mastering
son of my mother,
who bound me safely in bonds.

LOGE.
But, Mime, to bind thee
what bred him the might?

MIME.
With evil wit
welded Alberich,
of gold he wrung
from the Rhine, a ring;
at its stubborn spell
we stammer and stumble;
with it bridles he all
of us Nibelungs now to his bent.—

Once in our forges
freely we welded
gifts for our women,
winningest gear;
neatly like Niblungs we toiled,
and laughed for love of the time.
Now hotly he works us
in holes and in hollows;
for him alone
we hammer and live.
Through the golden ring
his greed can guess
what ore unhewn
is withheld in the earth;
then straight we must strike it,
grovel and stir it;
we smelt the booty
and smite at the bars,
without room or rest,
to heap our ruler the hoard.

LOGE.

What laggard was latest
under his lash?

MIME.

He looks on me,
alas! without mercy;
a helm he wished
heedfully welded;
he hinted well
the way he would have it.
I marked in mind
what boundless might
must be in the work,
as I wove the brass;
so, hoped to save
the helm for myself,
and in its force
from Alberich's fetter be free—
perhaps, yes perhaps,

outwit my unwearying heeder—
with fetters to rise and befall him—
the ring wrench from his finger—
so that; then, such as I find him,
a master in me he might feel!

LOGE.
What let thy wisdom
limp by the way?

MIME.
Ah, though the helm I had welded,
the wonder, that in it hides,
I read not aright how to hit!
 Who bespoke the work,
 and spoiled it away,
 he led me to learn,
 when truly too late,
what a trick lurked in the toy;
 from my face he faded,
 and blows, that from nowhere
known abounded, I bore.
 For such, my unthoughtful
 self I thank!
(*With cries, he rubs his back. The gods laugh.*)

LOGE
(*to Wotan*).
To seize, not light
at least he seems.

WOTAN.
But the foe, ere fail
thy wits, must fall.

MIME
struck with the laughter of the gods examines them more carefully).
Who are you that stir me
so strongly for answers?

LOGE.
Friends to thy kin;

we come to free
the Nibelungs forth from their need.
(*Alberich's scolding and beating approach again.*)

MIME.

Heed to yourselves!
He is at hand!

WOTAN.

We wait for him here.

(*He seats himself quietly on a stone; Loge leans at his side. Alberich, who has taken the tarn-helm from his head and hung it in his girdle, with the swing of his whip drives before him a crowd of Nibelungs upwards from the lower hollow; they are laden with gold and silver treasure which, under Alberich's continued abuse and blame, they store all in a pile and so heap to a hoard.*)

ALBERICH.

To-wards! Away!
Hihi! Hoho!
Lazy lot,
here aloft
heighten the hoard!
Thou there! On high!
Hinder not thus!
Harassing herd,
down with it hither!
Am I to help you?
All of it here!

(*He suddenly sees Wotan and Loge.*)

Hi! Who beholds?
What walks this way?—
Mime! To me,
rubbishing rogue!
Ply'st thou thy tongue
with the trespassing pair?
Forth, thou failer!
Hence to thy forge and thy hammer!

(*With strokes of his whip he drives Mime in among the crowd of the Nibelungs.*)

Hi! to your work!
Wontedly hasten!

The Rhinegold.

Lighten below!
From the greedy places
pluck me the gold!
The whip shall dint you,
dig you not well!
If listlessly Mime
lets you be minded,
he hardly will shield
from my hand his shoulders;
that I lurk like a neighbour
when nobody looks,
enough he lately has learned.—
Linger you still?
Loiter and stay?

(*He draws his ring from his finger, kisses it, and stretches it threateningly out.*)

Shake in your harness,
you shameful herd;
fitly fear
the ruling ring!

With howling and crying, the Nibelungs, with Mime among them, disperse and slip, in all directions, down into the pits.)

ALBERICH
(*fiercely approaching Wotan and Loge*).
What hunt you here?

WOTAN.

From Nibelheim's hiding land
we lately in news have heard
of endless wonders
worked under Alberich,
and greed to behold them
gained thee hither thy guests.

ALBERICH.

Your grudge you ran
rather to glut;
such nimble guests
I know well enough.

LOGE.
Know me indeed,
drivelling dwarf?
What seems there, so
to bark at, in sight?
When low in cowering
cold thou lay'st,
who fetched thee light
and fostering fire,
ere Loge laughed to thee first?
What for were thy hammer,
had I not heated thy forge?
Kinsman I count thee,
and friend I became,—
I think but faulty thy thanks!

ALBERICH.
For light-elves now
is Loge's laughter,
and slippery love;
art thou fully their friend,
as once my own thou wert—
ha ha! behold!—
I fear no further their hate!

LOGE.
So me to hope in thou mean'st!

ALBERICH.
In thy falsehood freely,
not in thy faith!—
But at ease face I you all.

LOGE.
Lofty mood
has lent thee thy might;
great and grim
thy strength has grown.

ALBERICH.
See'st thou the hoard

my sullen host
set me on high?

LOGE.

Such harvest I never have known.

ALBERICH.

A daylight's deed,
of scanty deepness;
mighty measure
must it end in hereafter.

WOTAN.

How helps thee now such a hoard
in hapless Nibelheim,
where nought for wealth can be won?

ALBERICH.

Goods to gather
and hide when together,
helps me Nibelheim's night;
but from the hoard,
in the hollow upheaped,
unheard of wonders I wait for;
the world with all
its wideness my own is for ever.

WOTAN.

To thy kindness how will it come?

ALBERICH.

Though in listless breezes' breadth
above me you live,
laugh and love;
with golden fist
you gods I will fall on together!
As love no more to me belongs,
all that has breath
must be without her;
though gold was your bane,
for gold you blindly shall grapple.

On sorrowless heights
in happy sway
you hold yourselves;
and dark-elves
you look in their deepnesses down on;—
have heed!
Have heed!—
When first you men
have fall'n to my might,
shall your frisking women
who failed to be wooed,
though dead is love to the dwarf,
feed under force his delight.—
Hahahaha!
Hear you not how?
Have heed!
Have heed of the night and her host,
when Niblungs heave up the hoard
from depth and dark into day!

WOTAN
(vehemently).
The false, slandering fool!

ALBERICH.
What says he?

LOGE
(stepping between them).
Thy senses see to!

(To Alberich.)
Who of wonder is empty,
that haps on Alberich's work?
If half thou would'st meet from the hoard
should come as means it thy cunning,
of all I must own thee most mighty;
for moon and stars
and the sun in the middle
would, like everything other,
work but under thy will.
But weighty holds it my wisdom,

that the hoard's upheavers—
  the Nibelungs' host—
hold thee not in hate.
Thou hast raised fiercely a ring,
and fear rose on thy folk ;
  but say, in sleep
    a thief on thee slipped
and reft slily the ring,
in safety would ward thee thy wits ?

                ALBERICH.
The longest of head is Loge ;
    others holds he
    always unhinged ;
    if he were but wanted
    to help my work
    for heavy thanks,
how high were his thievish heart !—
    The safening helm
    I hit on myself,
    the heedfullest smith,
Mime, had it to hammer ;
    ably to alter
    whither I aim,
    to be held for another,
    helps me the helm ;
    neighbours see me
    not when they search ;
    but everywhere am I,
    unsighted by all.
    So at my ease
I settle at even thy side,
my fond unslackening friend !

                LOGE.
    Life I have looked on,
    much have been led to,
    but such a wonder
    not once I have seen.
    The helm to believe in
    hardly I hasten ;

if thou hast told me truly,
for thy might is there no measure.

ALBERICH.

Deem'st thou I lie
and drivel like Loge?

LOGE.

Weight it with work,
or, dwarf, I must doubt thy word.

ALBERICH.

The blockhead with wind
of his wisdom will burst;
now grip thee thy grudge!
For say, in what kind of a shape
shall I come to thy sight?

LOGE.

The most to thy mind;
but dumb must make me the deed!

ALBERICH
(has put on the helm).

"Wheeling worm
wind and be with him!"

(He immediately disappears; in his place an enormous snake is seen winding on the ground; it rears and stretches its open jaws towards Wotan and Loge.)

LOGE
(pretends to be seized with fear).

Oho! Oho!
Snap not so fiercely,
thou fearful snake!
Leave my life to me further!

WOTAN
(laughs).

Right, Alberich!
Right, thou rascal!
How deftly waxed
the dwarf to the width of the worm!

(The snake disappears, and in its place Alberich immediately is seen again in his real form.)

ALBERICH.

How now! you doubters,
did I enough?

LOGE.

My fear is fully the witness.
The clumsy worm
becam'st thou at once
since what I watched,
thy word I take for the wonder.
But works it likewise
when to be little
and light thou wantest?
A safer trick were such,
in time of danger or dread;
only too deep after all!

ALBERICH.

Too deep indeed
it sounds for a dunce!
How slight shall I seem?

LOGE.

That the closest cleft may befit thee,
a toad can take to in fear.

ALBERICH.

Nought is lighter!
Look at me now!
(He puts the tarn-helm on again.)
"Grizzly toad
twist and grovel!"

(He disappears; the gods perceive among the stones a toad creeping towards them.)

LOGE
(to Wotan).
Trap with fleetest
fetter the toad!

Wotan puts his foot on the toad; Loge grasps at its head and seizes the tarn-helm in his hand.)

ALBERICH

(*becomes suddenly visible in his real shape as he writhes under Wotan's foot*).
Oho! Be cursed!
Behold me corded!

LOGE.

Tread him hard,
till he is tied.

(*He has taken out a rope and with it fastens Alberich's arms and legs; they both seize him as he writhes in his attempts to defend himself, and drag him with them towards the cleft by which they had descended.*)

LOGE.

Now swiftly up!
So he is ours!

(*They disappear upwards.*)

(*The scene gradually changes back to the*
OPEN DISTRICT ON MOUNTAIN HEIGHTS,
*as in the second scene; it is however still veiled in a pale mist, as, before the second change, after Freia's disappearance.
Wotan and Loge, dragging with them Alberich in his bonds, come up out of the cleft.*)

LOGE.

Here, kinsman,
come to thy halt!
Watch, belovèd,
and learn the world
thou wilt bend to thy beggarly will;
bespeak the spot,
where Loge his life may spend.

ALBERICH.

Rascally robber!
Thou wretch! Thou rogue!
Loosen the rope,
let me alone,
or pay at the last for thy pastime.

WOTAN.

With fetters hast thou

fairly been haltered,
since to the world,
that wheels and slides,
thou meantest thy will for master.
In fear thou art tied at my feet,
and feel'st the truth as I tell it;
thy wriggling limbs
now loose with a ransom.

ALBERICH.
Fie! the dunce,
the fool for my dream!
To think of trust
in the treacherous thieves!
Withering vengeance
wipe out the whim!

LOGE.
Ere vengeance befall us
thou first must vaunt thyself free;
to a foe in fetters
pay the free for no plunder.
So for vengeance to find us,
veer from thy fierceness
and reach us a ransom in full!

ALBERICH
(sharply).
Unfold what fix you to have?

WOTAN.
The hoard and thy glancing gold.

ALBERICH.
Wretched and ravening rogues!
(To himself.)
Yet let me but hold the ring,
the hoard without risk I can lose;
for again it shall gather
and sweetly shall grow
in the might of the mastering gold;

and the trick were a way
of turning me wise,
no further than fittingly paid,
if for it I part with the pile.

WOTAN.

The hoard shall we have?

ALBERICH.

Loosen my hand
and let it be here.

(*Loge unties his right hand.*)

ALBERICH

(*touches the ring with his lips and mutters the command*).
—And now the Nibelungs
hastily near;
my behest they bend to;
hark how they bring
from the deepness the hoard into day.
Now free me from press of the bonds!

WOTAN.

No bit till first thou hast paid.

(*The Nibelungs rise out of the cleft laden with the treasure of the hoard.*

ALBERICH.

O withering wrong—
that the wary rascals
should see me suffer such woe!—
Settle it here!
Hark what I say!
Strait and high
stow up the hoard!
Move it not lamely,
and look not at me!—
Downwards deep
at once from the daylight!
Back to the work
that waits in your burrows!

Harm to him that is faint,
for I fast shall follow you home!

(*The Nibelungs, after they have piled up the hoard, slip eagerly down again into the cleft.*)

ALBERICH.

The gold I leave you;
now let me go;
and the helm at least
that Loge withholds,
again you will give me for luck?

LOGE
(*throwing the tarn-helm on the hoard*).

By rights it belongs to the ransom.

ALBERICH.

The cursed thief!—
But comes a thought!
Who aided in one,
he welds me another;
still hold I the might
that Mime must heed.
Yet ill it feels
that eager foes
should have such a harbouring fence.—
But lo! Alberich
all has left you;
so loose the bite of his bonds!

LOGE
(*to Wotan*).

Now is he needless,
here in his knots?

WOTAN.

A golden hoop
behold on thy finger;
hear'st thou, dwarf?
Without it the hoard is not whole.

ALBERICH
(*horrified*).

The ring?

WOTAN.

Along with the ransom's
rest thou must leave it.

ALBERICH.

My life—ere I lose the ring!

WOTAN.

The ring I look for;
thou art welcome well to thy life!

ALBERICH.

Rendered, with breath and body,
the ring must be to the ransom;
    hand and head,
    eye and ear,
    are my own no rather
than here is this ruddy ring!

WOTAN.

Thy own thou wilt reckon the ring?
Ravest thou openly of it?
    Soundly here to me
    say whence thou hadst
the gold for the glimmering hoop?
    Ere thou torest it
    to thee under
the water, was it thy own?
    From the river's daughters
    rightfully draw
    whether the gold
    was so willingly given
from which the ring thou hast wrenched.

ALBERICH.

Sputtering slander!
Slovenly spite!
    Me to blot
    with the blame thy mind
so much was set on itself!

How long wouldst thou
have wished to leave them their wealth,
    hadst thou not held
the wisdom to weld it too hard?
    And well, thou feigner,
    fell it that once,
    when the Niblung here
    was gnawed to the heart
    at a nameless harm,
on the harrowing wonder he happed,
whose work now laughs to thy look!
    By woe seized upon,
    searched and wildered,
    a deed of crowded
    curses I did—
    and dreadly to-day
    shall the fruit of it deck thee,
my curse to befriend thee be called?
    Guard thyself more,
    masterful god!
    Wrought I amiss,
I wrecked but a right of mine;
but on all that will be,
    is and was,
god, thou raisest a wrong,
if got from my grasp is the ring!

        WOTAN.

    Off with the ring!
    No right to it
takest thou out of thy tongue.

(*With impetuous force he pulls the ring from Alberich's finger.*)

        ALBERICH
    (*with horrible shrieks*).

So! Uprooted! and wrecked!
Of wretches the wretchedest slave!

        WOTAN
(*has put the ring on his finger and gazes on it with satisfaction*).

And lo what makes me at last
of masters the mastering lord!

LOGE.

Leave has he got?

WOTAN.

Let him go!

LOGE
(*unfastens Alberich's bands*).
Haste to thy home!
Not a link withholds thee;
fare freely below!

ALBERICH
(*raising himself from the ground, with raging laughter*).
So am I free?
Safely free?—
Then fast and thickly
my freedom's thanks shall flow!—
As by curse I found it first,
a curse rest on the ring!
Gave its gold
to me measureless might,
now deal its wonder
death where it is worn!
No gladness grows
where it has gone,
and with luck in its look
it no more shall laugh;
care to his heart
who has it shall cleave,
and who holds it not
shall the need of it gnaw!
All shall gape
for its endless gain;
but wield it shall none
from now as wealth;
by its lord without thrift it shall lie,
but shall light the thief to his throat!
To death under forfeit,
faint in its dread he shall feel;

though long he live—
day by day he shall die,
and serve the ring
that he seems to rule;
till again its gold
I shall find and fill with my finger!—
Such blessing
in blackest need
the Nibelung has for his hoard!—
Withhold it now,
next to thy heart;
till my curse catches thee home!
(*He disappears quickly into the cleft.*)

LOGE.
So he leaves us
and sends his love!

WOTAN
(*lost in contemplation of the ring*).
Losing his spittle in spite!
(*The mist in the foreground gradually becomes clearer.*)

LOGE
(*looking towards the right*).
Fasolt and Fafner
haste from afar;
Freia follows their heels.
(*From the other side come in Fricka, Donner, and Froh.*)

FROH.
So back they are brought.

DONNER.
Be welcome, brother.

FRICKA
(*hurrying anxiously to Wotan*).
Sound will thy tidings sweetly?

LOGE
(*pointing to the hoard*).
Of trick and of force
the fruit we took,
and won what Freia wants.

DONNER.
From the giants' hold
joys she to hasten.

FROH.
With freshening breath
filled is my face ;
sweetness of sunlight
into me sinks !
Our hearts were wistful as women's
while here we waited for her,
who only yields us the bliss
of endlessly blossoming youth.

(*The foreground has again become bright ; the gods' appearance regains in the light its former freshness ; over the background, however, the mist still hangs, so that the distant castle remains invisible.*)

(*Fasolt and Fafner approach, leading Freia between them.*)

FRICKA
(*rushes joyously towards her sister to embrace her*).
Loveliest sister,
sweetest delight !
Bind me again to thy bosom !

FASOLT
(*forbidding her*)
Stay ! Let her alone !
Still she all is ours.—
At Riesenheim's
towering rim
rested we two ;
in blameless plight
the bargain's pledge
we held for pay ;
though grief it prove,
again we give her,
if whole and ready
the ransom's here.

WOTAN.
At hand lies it ready ;
in friendly mood
may it fairly be measured !

FASOLT.

To leave the woman,
lightly will lead me to woe;
so that she wane from my senses,
must the hoard we take
heighten its top,
till from my gaze
her flowering face it shall guard!

WOTAN.

At Freia's height
the heap shall be fixed.

(*Fafner and Fasolt stick their stakes in front of Freia into the ground, in such manner that they include the same height and breadth as her figure.*)

FAFNER.

The poles we have set
to the pledge's size;
the hoard must hide her from sight.

WOTAN.

Hurry the work;
hateful I hold it!

LOGE.

Help me, Froh!

FROH.

Freia's harm
haste I to finish.

(*Loge and Froh quickly heap the treasure between the stakes.*)

FAFNER.

Not so light
and loose it must look;
fast and firm
let it be found!

With rude force he presses the treasure close together; he stoops down to search for spaces.)

A gap I behold;
the holes are forgotten!

LOGE.
Withhold, thou lubber!
Lift not a hand!

FAFNER.
But look! A cleft to be closed!

WOTAN
(turning away in disgust).
Right to my heart
hisses the wrong.

FRICKA
(with her eyes fixed on Freia).
See how in shame
she shyly and sweetly shrinks;
to be loosed she lifts
wordless woe in her look.
O harmful man!
So much at thy hand she has met!

FAFNER.
Still more I miss!

DONNER.
Beside myself
makes me the wrath
roused by the mannerless rogue!—
Behold, thou hound!
Must thou measure,
thy size thou shalt settle with me!

FAFNER.
Softly, Donner!
Roll when thy sound
will help thee sooner than here!

DONNER.
With thy bark see if thou balk it!

WOTAN.
Hold thy rage!—
Already Freia is hid.

LOGE.

The hoard is drained.

FAFNER
(measuring with his eye).
Still dazzles me Holda's hair ;
more is at hand
meet for the heap !

LOGE.

Mean'st thou the helm ?

FAFNER.

Quickly let it come !

WOTAN.

Keep it not longer !

LOGE
(throws the helm on the heap).
Enough it is heightened.—
Now are you happy ?

FASOLT.

Freia's no longer
free to my look ;
is she then loosed ?
Am I to leave her ?

(He steps close up to the hoard and spies through it.)

Woe ! yet gleams
her glance to me well ;
her eyelight's star
streams without end ;
here through a cleft
it comes to me whole !—
While with her look I am lighted,
from the woman I will not loose.

FAFNER.

Hi ! what bring you
its brightness to hinder ?

LOGE.

Hunger-holder!
Hast thou forgot
that gone is the gold?

FAFNER.

Not fully, friend!
From Wotan's finger
glean the glimmering ring,
and choke the chink in the ransom.

WOTAN.

What! with the ring?

LOGE.

Madly mean you!
To Rhine-maidens
belongs its gold;
to their guard back he must give it.

WOTAN.

What blab'st thou about?
With work and wear I found it,
and freely save it myself.

LOGE.

Ill then weighs
it all for the word
that I gave them over their grief.

WOTAN.

But thy word can bar not my right;
as booty wear I the ring.

FAFNER.

But here for ransom
hast thou to reach it.

WOTAN.

Fleetly fix what you will;

all shall await you;
but all the world
not rend me out of the ring!

FASOLT.
(with rage pulls Freia from behind the hoard).
Then all is off,
the time is up,
and Freia forfeit for ever!

FREIA.
Help me! Hold me!

FRICKA.
Stubborn god,
stay not the gift!

FROH.
Gone let the gold be!

DONNER.
Hold not the hoop back!

WOTAN.
Leave me at rest!
I loose not the ring.

(Fafner still holds off the impetuous Fasolt; all stand in perplexity; Wotan in rage turns away from them. The stage has again become dark; from the chasm at the side a bluish light breaks forth; in it Wotan suddenly perceives Erda, who, as far as her middle, rises out of the depth; she is of noble appearance with wide-flowing black hair.)

ERDA
(stretching her hand warningly towards Wotan).
Yield it, Wotan, yield it!
Keep not what is cursed!
 Soon is sent
  darkly and downwards
he who saves the hoop.

WOTAN.
What warning woman is here?

ERDA.
How all has been, count I ;
how all becomes,
and is hereafter,
tell I too ;
the endless world's
ere-Wala,
Erda, bids thee bethink.
Thrice of daughters,
ere-begotten,
my womb was eased,
and so my knowledge
sing to thee Norns in the night-time.
But dread of thy harm
draws me in haste
hither to-day ;
hearken ! hearken ! hearken !
Nothing that is ends not ;
a day of gloom
dawns for the gods ;—
be ruled and wince from the ring !

She sinks slowly up to the breast, while the bluish light begins to darken.

WOTAN.
With hiding weight
is holy thy word ;
wait till I more have mastered !

ERDA
(*as she disappears*).
I warned thee now—
thou know'st enough ;
brood, and the rest forebode !
(*She disappears completely*.)

WOTAN.
Fear must sicken and fret me ?
Not if I seize thee,
and search to thy knowledge.

He attempts to follow Erda into the cleft to hold her ; Donner, Froh, and Fricka throw themselves before him and prevent him.)

The Rhinegold.

FRICKA.

What mischief maddens thee?

FROH.

Beware, Wotan!
Hallow the Wala,
hark to her word!

DONNER
(to the giants).

Heed, you giants!
Withhold your hurry;
the gold have, that you gape for.

FREIA.

How shall I hope it?
Was then Holda
rightly her ransom's worth?
(All look with anxiety at Wotan.)

WOTAN
(was sunk in deep thought and now collects himself with force to a decision).

To me, Freia!
I make thee free;
yield us again
the youth that thy going had reft!
You giants, joy of your ring!
(He throws the ring on the hoard.)
(The giants let Freia go; she hastens joyfully towards the gods, who for some time caress her by turns in greatest delight.)
(Fafner spreads out an immense sack and attacks the hoard to pack it in it.)

FASOLT
(throwing himself in his brother's way).

Softly, hungerer!
Some of it hither!
Both for a wholesome
half were the better.

FAFNER.

More to the maid than the gold
hadst thou not given thy heart?

F

With toil I brought
thy taste to the bargain.
Would'st thou have wooed
but half of Freia at once?
Halve I the hoard,
rightly I hold
the roundest sack for myself.

FASOLT.

Slandering rogue!
Rail at me so?
(*To the gods.*)
Try the matter between us;
halve for us meetly
here the hoard!
(*Wotan turns contemptuously away.*)

LOGE.

The rest leave to Fafner;
light with thy fist on the ring!

FASOLT

(*falls upon Fafner, who meanwhile has been vigorously packing his sack*).
Withhold, thou meddler!
Mine is the hoop;
I got it for Freia's glance.
(*He grasps sharply at the ring.*)

FAFNER.

Forth with thy fist!
My right is first!
(*They struggle; Fasolt wrenches the ring from Fafner.*)

FASOLT.

Mine wholly have I made it!

FAFNER.

Hold it fast! Might it not fall?
(*He strikes madly at Fasolt with his stake, and stretches him, with a blow on the ground; as he dies he snatches the ring from him.*)

Now freely at Freia blink;
with the ring at rest I shall be!

He puts the ring in the sack, and then leisurely packs the whole hoard.
All the gods stand horrified. Long solemn silence.)

WOTAN.

Fiercely comes
before me the curse's force!

LOGE.

Thy luck, Wotan,
will not be likened!
Much was reaped
when thou met'st with the ring:
but its good is still greater
since it is gone,
for their fellows, see,
slaughter thy foes
for the gold that thou forego'st.

WOTAN
(deeply moved).

Still misgivings unstring me!
A threatening fear
fetters my thought;
how to end it
Erda shall help me;
to her down I must haste!

FRICKA
(pressing caressingly to him).

What weighs on Wotan?
Sweetly await
the soaring walls
to draw with welcome
wide and warmly their doors.

WOTAN.

I bought with blameful
pay the abode!

DONNER

(pointing to the background, which is still veiled in mist).

Harassing warmth
hangs in the wind;
ill for breath
is the burdened air;
its lowering weight
shall lighten with scattering weather,
to sweep the sky for me sweet.

He has mounted a high rock in the slope of the valley, and begins to swing his hammer.)

Heyda! Heyda!
To me with you, mists!
In crowd at my call!
Hark how your lord
hails for his host!
At the hammer's swing
sweep to me here!
Heyda! Heyda!
Deepen the dark!
Donner hails for his host!

(The clouds have drawn themselves round him together; he disappears entirely in a mass of storm-cloud that gradually becomes denser and darker. Then the blow of his hammer is heard falling heavily on the rock; strong lightning leaps from the cloud; a violent thunder-clap follows.)

Brother, to me!
Mark out its way for the bridge!

(Froh has disappeared with him in the cloud. Suddenly it draws asunder; Donner and Froh become visible; from their feet, in blinding brightness, a rainbow bridge stretches over the valley to the castle, that now, lighted by the evening sun, shines in clearest splendour.)

(Fafner, near his brother's corpse, having at last packed the whole hoard into the great sack, has, during Donner's storm-spell, put it on his back and left the stage.)

FROH.

Though built lightly looks it,
fast and fit is the bridge;
it helps your feet
without fear to the hall!

WOTAN.

Evening eyelight
aims the sun;
its sinking stream
strikes widely the walls;
when they led the morning's
look into laughter,
lone and masterless,
lost and luring they lay.
From morning to evening,
with easeless mind
and might worked I to win them!
The night is near;
her hatred now
ward from my head the walls!
So—hail to the hall!
Shelter from shame and harm!

(To Fricka.)

Follow me, wife!
To Walhall find we the way!

(He takes her hand.)

FRICKA.

What sense is inside it?
The name till now was unsounded.

WOTAN.

What, in might over fear,
my manfulness found,
shall matchlessly live
and lead the meaning to light!

Wotan and Fricka walk towards the bridge; Froh and Freia follow next, then Donner.)

LOGE

(lingering in the foreground and looking after the gods).

To their end they fleetly are led,
who believe themselves founded for ever.
Almost I shame
to mix in their matters;

in flustering fire
afresh to be loosened
a lurking fondness I feel.
To swallow the teachers
who settled me tame,
rather than blindly
blend in their wreck,
though godliest gods I may think them,
no fool's thought were it found!
I'll deem about it;
who bodes what I do?

(*He proceeds leisurely to join the gods. Out of the depth is heard the song of the Rhine-daughters, sounding upwards.*)

THE THREE RHINE-DAUGHTERS.

Rhinegold!
Guiltless gold!
How bright and unbarred
was to us once thy beam!
We mourn thy loss
that lone has made us!
Give us the gold,
O bring us the gleam of it back!

WOTAN

(*just about to set his foot on the bridge, stops and turns round*).
Whose sorrow reaches me so?

LOGE.

The river-maidens',
who grieve for their missing gold.

WOTAN.

The cursed Nodders!—
Keep me clear of their noise!

LOGE

(*calling down into the valley*).
You in the water,
why yearn you and weep?
Hear from Wotan a hope—

"Gleams no more
"the gold to the maids,
"may the gods, with strengthened glory,
"sun them sweetly instead!"

(The gods laugh aloud and step on to the bridge.)

THE RHINE-DAUGHTERS
(from the depth).

Rhinegold!
Guiltless gold!
O would that thy light
in the wave had been left alive!
Trustful and true
is what dwells in the depth;
faint and false
of heart what is happy on high

(As all the gods are crossing the bridge to the castle, the curtain falls.)

FIRST DAY.

THE WALKYRIE.

PERSONS.

SIEGMUND.
HUNDING.
WOTAN.
SIEGLINDE.
BRÜNNHILDE.
FRICKA.
Eight Walkyries.

THE WALKYRIE.

FIRST ACT.

The inside of a dwelling-place. (In the middle stands the stem of a mighty ash, whose roots in strong relief straggle far over the ground; the top of the tree is shut out by a wooden roof pierced in such a manner that the stem and the branches, which stretch in every direction, pass through corresponding openings; it is assumed that the foliage of the top spreads itself out above this roof. Built round the ash-stem as centre is a wooden room; the walls are of rough-hewn woodwork hung here and there with woven curtains. To the right in the foreground stands the hearth, the chimney of which goes sideways out through the roof; behind the hearth is an inner room like a store-house to which a few wooden steps lead up; before it hangs a woven curtain half drawn back. In the background an entrance-door with smooth wooden bolt. To the left the door of an inner chamber, to which also steps lead up; further forward on the same side a table, with a broad wooden seat behind it attached to the wall, and with wooden footstools in front of it.)
(A short orchestral prelude of impetuous stormy movement introduces the action. As the curtain rises, Siegmund hurriedly opens the entrance-door from without and comes in; it is towards evening; a strong storm just about to end. Siegmund holds for a moment the bolt in his hand and surveys the room; he appears spent with extreme exertion; his clothes and looks show that he is in flight. As he sees no one he shuts the door behind him, walks to the hearth and throws himself exhausted on a covering of bearskin.)

SIEGMUND.
Whose hearth here may be,
help it must bring me.

(He sinks back and remains for some time stretched out without movement. Sieglinde enters from the door of the inner chamber. From the noise she had heard she supposed it was her husband returned home; her look expresses earnest surprise at seeing a stranger stretched out at the hearth.)

SIEGLINDE
(still in the background).
An unknown man!
Me he must answer.

(She goes softly a few steps nearer.)

Who haunts the house
and lies at the hearth?

(*As Siegmund does not move she goes still a little nearer and looks at him.*)

Weary looks he
with length of way;—
seized him a sickness?
Lost is his sense?

(*She bends closer to him.*)

He breathes with his bosom;
his lids he but lowered;—
meet and manful he seems,
in his sunken might.

SIEGMUND
(*suddenly raising his head*).

A well! a well!

SIEGLINDE.

I go for water.

(*She hurriedly takes a drinking horn, goes out of the house, comes back with it filled and hands it to Siegmund.*)

Drink, to ease it,
I offer thy dryness;
water—what thou hast wished!

(*Siegmund drinks and hands the horn back to her. After he has made signs of thanks with his head, his look remains fixed with growing sympathy on her features.*)

SIEGMUND.

Fast with its coolness
filled me the cup,
a lifted weight
lightens my limbs,
my mood is a man's,
my eye is wide
with wonted sweetness of sight;
who wakes and welcomes me so?

SIEGLINDE.

The woman and house
are wealth of Hunding;

let him lend thee his roof;
halt till he reaches home!

SIEGMUND.

Weaponless am I;
the wounded guest
he will grieve not to harbour.

SIEGLINDE
(anxiously).
But where are hidden thy hurts?

SIEGMUND
(shakes himself and springs vigorously up into a sitting posture).
Too light weigh they
to lead to a word;
my limbs in their sockets
safely are left.
If but half as well as my hands
shield and weapon had helped me,
flight from foes I had shunned;
but in shivers they falsely fell.
The foe with his hatred
followed me hard,
a burning storm
stifled my breath;
but faster than I could fly them,
wanes my faintness away;
lost is the night from my look,
and sunlight sent me anew.

SIEGLINDE
(has filled a horn with mead and hands it to him).
The freshening might
of flowery mead
seek not to leave unsipped.

SIEGMUND.
First if it feel thy lips!

(Sieglinde sips the horn and offers it to him again; Siegmund takes a long draught; he then takes the horn quickly from his lips and gives it back. They look at each other for some time in silence and with increasing interest.)

SIEGMUND
(*with trembling voice*).
With thy help met'st thou a hapless man;—
far may woe
from thy way be found!
(*He starts quickly up to depart.*)
Aroused and rested
and sweetly saved,
forth from sight I will fare.

SIEGLINDE
(*turning quickly round*).
Who besets thee to flee so soon?

SIEGMUND
(*stayed by her voice turns again; slowly and gloomily*).
Ill-luck I always
after me lead;
ill-luck is swiftly
lured where I settle;
but aloof from thy side it shall light!
Forth lift I look and foot.
(*He goes quickly to the door and lifts the bar.*)

SIEGLINDE
(*calling after him with impetuous self-forgetfulness*).
Here stay behind!
No sorrow hast thou for her,
whose house is her sorrow's seat!

SIEGMUND
(*deeply moved remains standing and searches Sieglinde's face; she at length, ashamed and sad, casts down her eyes. Long silence. Siegmund turns back and sits down leaning against the hearth*).
Wehwalt—I said that I was;—
Hunding here I will wait for.

(*Sieglinde remains in troubled silence; then starts, listens and hears Hunding lead his horse to the stable outside; she goes hastily to the door and opens it.*)

(Hunding, armed with shield and spear, appears and remains standing in the doorway when he sees Siegmund.)

SIEGLINDE
(in reply to Hunding's seriously inquiring look).
Faint at the hearth
I found him here;
harm followed him fast.

HUNDING.
Thou fresh'ned'st him?

SIEGLINDE.
His mouth I moistened him,
gladly made him guest.

SIEGMUND
(steadily and quietly observing Hunding).
House and drink
I had from her;
blame shall it help to bring her?

HUNDING.
Holy is my hearth;—
holy find thou my house!
(To Sieglinde, as he puts off his weapons and hands them to her.)
Haste the meal for us men!
(Sieglinde hangs up the weapons on the ash-stem, takes food and drink out of the store-room and sets supper on the table.)

HUNDING.
(examines sharply and with surprise Siegmund's features, which he compares with his wife's; to himself).
How like to the woman!
The lurking worm
looms like hers in his look.
(He conceals his surprise, and turns without restraint to Siegmund.)
Long thy way
looks to have wound;
no horse he rode,
who rested here;
what muddy pathways
made thee thy pain?

SIEGMUND.
Through field and forest,
heather and hedge,
hunted me storm
and strongest need;
I know not the way that I went;
where I have lighted
learned I of none;
gladly I'd gather the news.

HUNDING
(at the table, and offering Siegmund a seat).
Whose house thou hast,
whose roof's thy rest,
Hunding reckon the host:
well to the westward
from here away,
in crowded halls
harbour the kindred,
who foster the fame of Hunding.
Make me glad of my guest;
let me greet him now by his name!

(Siegmund, who has seated himself at the table, fixes his eyes in thought. Sieglinde has seated herself by Hunding, opposite Siegmund, and fastens her look on the latter with strange sympathy and expectation.)

HUNDING
(watching them both).
May not the truth
be trusted with me,
my wife shall take thy tidings;
see how she waits for their sound!

SIEGLINDE
(with unembarrassed sympathy).
Guest, of thy name
I gladly would know.

SIEGMUND
(raises his eyes, looks in her face, and begins earnestly).
Friedmund I cannot be called;
Frohwalt would that I were;
but to Wehwalt only I answer.

Wolfe my father was;
at once into the world
awoke a sister and I;
   soon missed I
   both mother and maid;
   who brought me forth—
   and who fellowed my birth;
barely I knew them by name.
Warlike and strong was Wolfe;
his foes unstinted and fierce.
   Once forth to hunt
   my father I followed;
   from hurry and heat
   when homeward he led,
left we beheld the lair;
   to dust was burnt
   the lordly abode,
   to a stump the oak's
   unwithering stem,
   before us the mother
   manfully fall'n,
   and smothered in cinders
   the sister's trace;—
the Neidings' treacherous band
had dealt us the deadly blow.
   Beset we fled—
   the father and son;
   years now lurked
   the life of the youngling
with Wolfe in wild and wood;
   hunt and snare
   were set for their heels;
   but well we warded them—
   wolf and whelp.
     (Turning to Hunding.)
A Wölfing tells thee the tale,
who as "Wölfing" follows his fame.

     HUNDING.
Wonder and startling story,
stranger, thy words unwind;

Wehwalt—the Wölfing!
In tidings of wildness and war
their names ere now were told me,
    though never I Wolfe
    and Wölfing knew.

SIEGLINDE.

But further, guest, unfold
where to-day thy father dwells.

SIEGMUND.

The Neidings fiercelier now
held us in hunt than before;
    the wolf was hard
    with wounds on his hunters,
    in flight from their game
    fast they were gone;
they sped before us like spray.
But my father amid them I missed,
    and his track was fainter
    the further I trod;
    a fallen wolfskin
    far in the wood
I found under my feet;
my father I met no more.
When the wood wanted his face,
it forced me to men and to women;—
    wherever I fared,
    whomever I found,
    wished I for friend,
    or strove for wife,—
still was my wooing unwanted;
ill-luck on me lay.
The rule I counted right—
others cried to be wrong;
the deed I deemed was false—
others found to be fair,
    and war was with me
    over the world;

      rage rose
      on every road;
      grasped I at gladness,
      woe was my gain;
so to call myself Wehwalt came I,
for only woe was my own.

HUNDING.

To have let thee know such luck,
must love thee not the Norn;
with gladness hails thee no host
to whom thou go'st as guest.

SIEGLINDE.

None but cowards mind a man
unweaponed and lone to meet!—
      Yet further, guest,—
      why it befell
at last thy weapons were lost?

SIEGMUND
(with increasing animation).

A hapless child
      hailed me for help;
      her kin were minded
      to couple by might,
to a man that she loved not, the maid;
      heed to her grief
      I hastily gave;
      with scars and blood
      scattered the band;
the field I bared of foes;
undone and dead were the brothers;
the woman bewailed on their breasts;
her wrath was wrecked in her woe;
with tide too full to quench
befell the quarry her tears;
for their death, that herself she had dealt in,
sorrowed the brotherless bride.
      But a storm of kindred
      came as I stood,

vengeance swore
and vowed they would slaughter me
round us the forest
flamed with their faces;
still from the men
stirred not the maid;
with sword and spear
her safety I served,
till hilt and shaft
were hewn from my hand.
Wounded and shelterless was I—
saw them murder the maid;
I fled from the rage of the foe—
on the slaughter she rested slain.
(*With a look of painful fire at Sieglinde.*)
Now, asking woman, thou know'st
why is not—Friedmund my name!

(*He gets up and walks to the hearth. Sieglinde, deeply moved, turns pale and looks down.*)

HUNDING
(*very sullenly*).

I've heard of a bridleless breed,
not holy it holds
what others hail;
by men it is hated and me.
To help a vengeance I hasted;
blood of my kindred
from earth had called;
too late I came,
and hardly am back
when in house and hall I tread
on track of the flying foe.
My doors ward thee,
Wölfing, to-day;
till the dawn shelter they show;
a flawless sword
will befit thee at sunrise;
by day be ready for fight,
and pay thy debt for the dead.

To Sieglinde, who, with anxious gesture, places herself between the two men.

Hence from the hall!
Loiter not here!
The night-drink brew within,
and bide for me to bed.

(Sieglinde takes thoughtfully a drinking horn from the table, goes to a cupboard from which she takes spices, and turns towards the side-chamber; having reached the highest step by the door she turns once more and aims at Siegmund—who with suppressed rage stands quietly by the hearth and sees nothing but her—a long longing look with which, at last, she directs him meaningly and urgently to a spot in the ash-stem. Hunding, who notices her delay, drives her forth with a commanding gesture, whereupon, with the drink-horn and the lantern, she disappears through the doorway.)

HUNDING
(takes his weapons from the tree).

With weapons ward themselves men.
I meet thee, Wölfing, to-morrow;
thou heard'st what I said—
see to thyself!

(He goes with his weapons into the chamber.)

SIEGMUND
(alone—it has now become quite night; the room is only lighted by a faint fire in the hearth Siegmund sits down on the couch near the fire and broods for some time in troubled silence).

A sword, so swore me my father,
should be near me in furthest need.
Weaponless finds me
a house of foes;
here to their hate
in pledge I am held;
I saw a woman
lordly and sweet,
and gladness sets
its dread in my soul;—
to her here my pulses pour,
with the sway of sweetness she pulls—
a husband holds her in might,
who mocks my weaponless hand.
Wälse! Wälse!
Where is thy sword?

The steadfast sword,
that in storm I would swing!
Breaks there not out of my breast
the rage that at heart I bear?

(The fire falls together; from the sparks, as they spring up, a sharp light falls on the spot in the ash-stem which Sieglinde's look had pointed out, and where now more plainly is seen the hilt of a sword.)

What firmly gleams
in the fitful glow?
How the blaze starts
from the ash's stem!
The steady lightning
strengthens its stare,—
stays and laughs like a look.
How the lordly light
my heart has lit!
Is it a flash
that her flowering face
can have left here
behind her at last,
when from the hall she went?

(The fire on the hearth begins gradually to go out.)

Settled shadow
shrouded my sight;
when the might of her look
lighted on me,
morning and warmth it awoke.
High and happy
the sun I beheld;
he filled with the light
of his laughter my face,—
till far he hid in the hills.
Again, ere all was gone,
he aimed an evening gleam
for the ash's fading stem
to answer in stately fire;
now falls the flower—
the light allays—
night in shade
has shut me anew;

deep in my bosom's darkness
hides an unbrightening heat !

(*The fire has quite gone out ; complete night. The side-chamber is lightly opened ; Sieglinde, in a white garment, comes out and goes towards Siegmund.*)

SIEGLINDE.

Sleep'st thou, guest ?

SIEGMUND.
(*leaping up with sudden joy*).
Who seeks me so ?

SIEGLINDE
(*with mysterious haste*).
It is I ; behold what I say !
In heedless sleep is Hunding ;
I set him a drink for his dreams.
The night for thy safety thou need'st !

SIEGMUND
(*fierily interrupting her*).
Safe makes me thy side !

SIEGLINDE.

To a weapon let me lead thee—
O were thy lot to win it,
    the highest hero
    lo I might hail thee,
    the man with the hand
    meant for its hilt.
O take with heed what I tell thee !
    By Hunding's kin
    was crowded the hall,
to help at the wine of his wedding ;
    the woman he married,
    against her will
wretches had given to wife.
    Drearly I sat
    aside from the drinkers ;
a stranger strode to the board—

in a cloak of blue he was clad,
  so wide was his hat,
that one of his eyes was hidden ;
  from its fellow's flash
  dreadly they faltered,
  when fell in their midst
  its unflinching might ;
  in me alone
  met was its light
with sweet wildering woe,
sorrow and salve at once.
  He gazed at me,
  and glared on the men,
as he heaved a sword in his hands,
  and aimed it straight
  at the ash's stem,
to the hilt hurried it in ;—
he only should have the weapon,
who hauled it from out the wood.
  Though most they made
  of their might in the work,
not a man the weapon could move ;—
  guests have gathered
  and guests have gone,
the strongest grasped at the steel—
not an inch they started it out ;
here still is settled the sword.
So guessed I who was he
that here had greeted my grief ;
  I know as well
  for none but one
he stuck the sword in the stem.
  O found I but now
  and near me his face,
  fared he this way
  to the friendless woman,
  the woe I have measured
  with merciless moans,
  the bonds that in shame
  and shade I have borne,—

sweetening vengeance
swiftly would swallow!
At last lit on
were all I have lost,
at once would be won
all I have wept for—
found I the holy friend
and felt him here at my heart!

SIEGMUND
(embraces her with fire).
So—free from thy sorrow
makes thee the friend
for weapon and woman meant!
Up from my breast
blazes the oath
that weds me all to thy worth.
Whatever I hoped for,
in thee I behold;
whatever failed me,
in thee I have found!
Wounded thee wrong
and wasted me woe—
have I been hunted—
with shame hast thou housed—
hastening vengeance
hails to me hither!
Loud I laugh
to greet its delight,
holding thee guarded and holy,
bearing the blow of thy heart!

SIEGLINDE
(starts in alarm and tears herself from him).
Ha! who went? who was it came?
(The large door in the background has sprung back and remains wide open; outside a splendid Spring night; the full-moon shines in and flings its light on them both, so that they suddenly and plainly see each other.)

SIEGMUND
(in gentle ecstasy).
No-one went—
but one has come;

The Walkyrie.

> look how the Spring
> laughs in the hall!

(With soft violence he draws her to himself on the couch.)

> Winter storms have waned
>   at the wakening May,
>   and mildly spreads
>   his splendour the Spring;
>   he buoys himself
>   on bending breezes,
>   wonders last
>   along his way;
>   over field and forest
>   floats his freshness,
>   wide with laughter
>   wakes his look.
> He sounds in boundless singing
>   of buoyant birds,
>   sweetening breath
>   his bosom swells;
> from his blood are warmed and wakened
>   wildering blossoms,
>   seed and shoot
>   from his heart he sends.
> With winsome weapons' flash
>   he forces the world;
> winter and storm have waned
>   at his steadfast war;
> with dint of his dreadless strokes
> the stubborn doors he has daunted,
>   whose hindering hinge
>   withheld us from him.

> To find his sister
>   he sets his flight,
> by Love was lured the Spring;
>   behind our hearts
>   she deeply was hid;
> now let her laugh to the light.

The bride and the sister
is free to the brother;
the walls are waste
that held them away;
greeting together
they shout as they go,
for Spring has lighted on Love!

SIEGLINDE.

Thou here art the spring
I hungered and hoped for
in withering winter's hold;
I hailed thee with holy
dread in my heart,
when thy look was first on me lifted.
Friendly was nothing I found,
far I felt what was nearest,
unknown and nameless what most
made its seat at my side;
at last clearly
cam'st thou, and lo
ere my eye from thee moved,
my own it had made thee;
what I hid in my heart,
all I am,
dawned like a sudden
day to my sight;
with sound of a storm
my ear was beset,
when in fruitless frosty loneness
at length on my friend I lit.

(*She hangs in transport on his neck and looks closely into his face.*)

SIEGMUND.

O wildering sweetness!
Sorrowless woman!

SIEGLINDE
(*close to his eyes*).

O let me clasp thee
and lock thee closely,

that long I may ponder
the lordly light,
whose blaze from thy face
and forehead breaks,
and so sweetly forces my sense!

   SIEGMUND.

The flooding moon
makes thee on fire,
deeply holds thee
thy heaving hair;
why I am wild
I learn from my look,
that feeds unfilled on thy face.

   SIEGLINDE.
(sweeps the hair back from his forehead and gazes at him with wonder).
How broad thou art
and open of brow,
how tangles the blood
in thy temples its boughs!
I flinch at the sweetness
that fills my sight—
a wonder sends me its warning;—
though first it neared me to-night,
thy face I knew before!

   SIEGMUND.

In dreams of love
thy like has loomed;
with burning sadness
such I have seen!

   SIEGLINDE.

My face I read
in the resting flood—
and here I further behold it;
as once from the water it shone,
show me my likeness thy looks!

   SIEGMUND.

In depth of my dream
thy face to me dawned.

SIEGLINDE
(suddenly turning away her look).
O stay—let me
be still and listen ;—
in childhood a sound
laughed to me so—
but hold ! for lately I heard it
give me again my shout,
when it had shaken the woods.

SIEGMUND.
O loveliest tones,
aloud to me linger !

SIEGLINDE
(suddenly again searching his eyes).
In thy glance's fire
I gladdened before,
when mutely the stranger's
streamed upon me,
till my sorrow was mild and sweet.
By his dauntless look
his daughter was led—
I longed with his name to be near him—
(She stops, and then proceeds softly.)
Wehwalt canst thou be called ?

SIEGMUND.
No longer, since
thy love I learned ;
my bliss at last is unbounded !

SIEGLINDE.
And is Friedmund not
the name that befits thee ?

SIEGMUND.
Give me the name
thou wert glad I should go by,
and only thy gift I will own !

SIEGLINDE.
Yet Wolfe thou callest thy father?

SIEGMUND.
A wolf among fainting foxes!
But he, who as far
flashed with his eyelight
as launches the aim of thy look,
for none but " Wälse " was known.

SIEGLINDE
(*beside herself*).
Was Wälse thy father,
and fronts me a Wolsung,
stuck he his sword
for thy sake in the stem
a name I have lit on
by which to love thee;
Siegmund—
lo is its sound!

SIEGMUND
(*springs to the stem and seizes the sword-hilt.*)
Siegmund is it,
and Siegmund I am
as settles the sword
I unflinchingly seize!
Wälse forewarned me,
in sorest woe
near I should have it—
I hold it now!
Want with its strongest
wildest stress,
love with its newest
loudest need,
burn me deep in the breast,
drive me to deeds and death!—
Nothung! Nothung
my weapon I name.—
Nothung! Nothung!
Sundering sword!

Bare me the shearing
shine of thy blade,
and sweep from thy sheath to me so!

(With a mighty wrench he draws the sword out of the stem and shows it to Sieglinde, who is seized with wonder and joy.)

Siegmund the Wolsung,
woman, thou see'st!
For bride-gift
this sword let him bring;
he well has won
the rightfullest wife;
her wrongful roof
at length he bereaves;
forth from here
follow him far;
speed to the laughing
house of the Spring,
where saves thee Nothung the sword,
since Siegmund to love thee has lived!

(He folds her in his arms, to take her forth with him.)

SIEGLINDE
(in highest ecstasy).

Siegmund art thou
safely beside me,
Sieglinde's longing
has led thee at last,
and so thy sister
thou winnest at once with the sword!

SIEGMUND.

Bride and sister
be to thy brother—
and blossom the Wolsungs' blood!

(He draws her to him with fiery force; she sinks with a cry on his breast. The curtain falls quickly.)

SECOND ACT.

A wild region of rocks. (In the background a ravine slopes up from below and issues on a high ridge, from which the ground again sinks downwards towards the foreground.)
(Wotan, armed in warlike manner, and with his spear; before him Brünnhilde, as Walkyrie, also fully armed.)

WOTAN.

To me with thy horse,
mettlesome maid!
Soon will blaze
of battle be seen;
Brünnhild' away to the strife,
and stir the Wolsung to win!
Hunding leave I
for him he delights;
to Walhall lies not his way.
So fitly and fast
ride to the fight!

BRÜNNHILDE
(shouting and springing from rock to rock up the height on the right).
Hoyotoho! Hoyotoho!
Heiaha! Heiaha!
Hahei! Hahei! Heiaho!

(She stops on a high point of rock, looks down into the ravine behind, and calls back to Wotan.)

For safety, father,
see to thyself;
heed the storm
that hitherward steers;
hunts thee Fricka thy wife—
this way she reins her harness of rams.
Hey! how she whirls
the golden whip;
the luckless beasts
unboundedly bleat;

her wheels wildly she rattles,
wrath is lit in her look.
　　I fail at such
　　a fight to be found;
　　more to my mind
　　are the battles of men!
Now judge how the storm thou wilt stem;
I leave thee with joy in the lurch!
　　Hoyotoho! Hoyotoho!
　　Heiaha! Heiaha!
Hahei! Hahei! Hoyohei!
(*She has disappeared behind the height at the side, while Fricka, in a chariot drawn by two rams, reaches the ridge; there she quickly alights and walks impetuously to Wotan in the foreground.*)

WOTAN
(*as he sees her coming*).
The wonted storm,
　　the wonted strife!
But here she steadfast beholds me.

FRICKA.
Where in heights thyself thou hid'st
away from sight of thy wife,
　　lonelily
　　I look for thee here,
that with help thou may swear to uphold
　　me.

WOTAN.
What Fricka frets at
let her unfold.

FRICKA.
I have learned Hunding's hurt;
aloud for vengeance he hailed,
　　and as wedlock's warder
　　I heard him well;
　　I vowed that sore
　　should pay for their sin
the mad mannerless pair,
who put the husband to harm.

Befriend me meetly,
that fast may their meed
upon Siegmund and Sieglinde fall.

WOTAN.

What so dreadful
was the deed
they did by spell of the Spring?
The might of love
had made them mad;
they bear not its wonder's blame!

FRICKA.*

Thou fittingly feign'st to be blind,
but better is known to none
that here, for wedlock's
holiest word
unbound and baffled, I hate them!

---

* *I give here in full the original form of this scene as it was conceived before the composition of the music.*

FRICKA.
Thou fittingly feign'st to be blind,
but better is known to none
how fierce a wrong
on Fricka has fallen
and hurts her at heart.

WOTAN.
Thou watchest but one thing;
I see another
that sets it out of my sight.

FRICKA.
I heed what always
I aimed to uphold,—
the worshipped oath of wedlock;
who sins against it,
he sickens my soul;
who harms it, he strikes at my heart.

WOTAN.
Is wedlock so lightly thy word,
where but fetters of love I can find?

The Walkyrie.

WOTAN.

Unholy
hold I the oath
where love lent not his hand;
so from me deem
no more of a deed,
that with might shall foil
what thou may'st not fancy;
for where fresh forces are stirring,
I sting them freely to strife.

Unholy
hold I the oath
where love lent not his hand.
Weak is made
a woman in worth,
when holy thou holdest the way
that Hunding went for a wife!

FRICKA.

If fierce force
blindly and far
wastes about us the world,
what rightly shall bear
the ruin's blame
but Wotan's wildering rage?
Weakness thou wilt not shelter,
and strength thou stay'st with thy shield;
mankind's madness
and savage mood,
murder and theft,
are things of thy might;
I labour to see that high
and holy something be left.
Where men from warfare
have weaned their mind,
where wealth is walled
that chafelessly weathers
the withering storm of change,—
I lurk and lightly watch.
The wielding cord
of a wounded wont
I bind again to a band;

Fricka.

Bear'st thou as boastworthy
wedlock's breach,
withhold not thy freedom—
but have it holy
that blood so should be blent
by twins in unseemly bond.
I falter at heart,
my head is on fire;
bridally seizes
brother on sister!
When—was it a man
should mate with the child of his mother?

---

with ruin beside me,
I draw from it so
the dew of holiest hope.
When Hunding fought
with a hand of force
that my weakness could not ward,
thou cam'st not to foil his freedom;
soon as he wiped
his sin away
by words of hallowing wedlock,
Fricka with friendship beheld him,
fast forgave
and forgot his fault,
and raised to shelter
his right her shield.
His deed at thy hand was unhindered,
so cross not my calm to-day!

Wotan.

When put I a stay
on the step of thy purpose,
or stood in way of thy will?
Narrow the belt
of binding knots,
girdle what fits not together,
feign peace,
and fill thy pride
over lying oaths of love;

WOTAN.
Here—haps it at last,
   and helps thee learn
   what is fair and fit,
though thou never hast known it before.
   The love of the couple
   is clear to thy look,
so trust my counsel for true!
   If lasting bliss
   shall belong to thy blessing,
with blameless laughter the lovers,
Siegmund and Sieglinde, bless!

   but from me deem
   no more of a deed,
   that with might shall foil
   what thou may'st not fancy;
for where fresh forces are stirring,
I sting them freely to strife.

     FRICKA.
Bear'st thou as boastworthy
   wedlock's breach,
   withhold not thy freedom—
   but have it holy
that blood so should be blent
by twins in unseemly bond.
   I falter at heart,
   my head is on fire;
   bridally seizes
   brother on sister!
When—was it a man
should mate with the child of his mother?

     WOTAN.
Here—haps it at last,
   and helps thee learn
   what is fair and fit,
though thou never hast known it before.

     FRICKA.
With heedless scorn
   behold'st thou my harm?
   To reckless laughter
   has led thee my wrath?

** FRICKA
(breaking out in fierce anger).
So is there an end
of our godhood for ever,
since thou thy guideless
Wolsungs begottest?
The track tread I—
strike I on truth?
The call of thy holy
kin is unheeded;

Wilt thou mock the worth,
thou mad'st with thy word?
Undo the worship
that dwells in thy wife?
Unfettered god,
how far wilt thou go?
Wilt thou scatter and waste the world
whose laws thyself thou hast laid?

WOTAN.

I wield, ere aught,
what of old was wonted;
where forces stream and struggle,
I fix the line of my labour;
whither it flows
I lead the flood,
and watch the fount
from which it is fed;
in the strength of limb and of love
I measure the right to live.
The might that moulded
the twins was mine;
the ways of love
they learned in the womb;
unwittingly clasped they were born,
to bridal unwittingly came.
If sweet is to be
the sway of thy blessing,
now bless, with unhindered
hallowing bent,
Siegmund's and Sieglinde's bond.

[*At* ** *continued in the text.*]

      away thou hurlest
      what once was hallowed;
      the bands that thou boundest
      thyself thou hast broken,
      loosed with laughter
      the heavens' hold—
for the cursed whim of a couple
of taunting and worthless twins,
thy own falsehood's unwarranted fruit!
      Vainly I wail to thee
      wedlock and vow
thou wert first thyself to unfix!
      My open truth
      was always betrayed;
      where was a height
      and where was a hollow
      that long lacked
      the lust of thy look
where to choose a change of delight
and scath my love with the scorn?
      Blankly myself
      I settled to bear it,
      when met thee for battle
      the blameful maidens
      thy lawless love
      had brought to the light,
for thy wife still boasted such worth,
      that the Walkyries' band
      with Brünnhild' to boot,
      thy wish's bride,
at my will to be guided thou gav'st.
      But now, that unwonted
      names thou hast wedded,
      as "Wälse" fared
      like a wolf in the forest;
      now, that to fathomless
      shame thou hast fallen,
      of common mankind
      begotten a couple,
sheer at the feet of the she-wolf's
litter at last I am flung!

So follow the mood,
measure it full,
the betrayed may meetly be trampled!

WOTAN
(calmly).

Thou would'st not take,
were I to tell thee,
a truth thou can'st never know
until its deed has been done.
Wonted things
are the way of thy thought;
but what was never before
I now fancy to wake!
To one thing hearken!
A hero we wait,
unshackled by gods with their shelter
and loose in the grasp of their law,
fitly forward
the work to befriend,
which, though by gods it is wanted,
the hand of a god may not help.

FRICKA.

With depth of dealing
seek not to daunt me!
What feat, that hands
of heroes are fit for,
could be forbidden their gods—
by whose gift alone they can live?

WOTAN.

Is their own mettle
not meet for aught?

FRICKA.

Who blew its might into men?
Who lighted its blaze in their look?
The strength they show
shoots from thy stay,
and at thy stinging
struggle they up:

thou—only hast urged them,
as bears me out thy own boast.
    With new untruth
    thou wilt now betray me,
    with tricks afresh
    thou triest to foil me;
    but here this Wolsung
    to win never hope;
in his behold I thy aim,—
at thy will only he works.

WOTAN.

    In need his saver
    was none but himself;
my hand hallowed him not.

FRICKA.

No further fence him now;
    have back the sword
    that thou sentest him!

WOTAN.

    The sword?

FRICKA.

    So—the sword,
    the stormy
    unstaggering sword,
that the god has given his son.

WOTAN.

    Siegmund won it
    himself in his want.

FRICKA.

    From Wotan, as well
    as the sword, was the want;
    deem'st thou I know not—
    when, day and night,
in dread I was hard at thy heels?

Whose strength for him stuck
the sword in the stem?
With the holy hilt
who filled his hand?
Thou can'st not count it
as aught but thy craft,
that warned him where it was kept!

(*Wotan makes a gesture of rage.*)

With bondsmen
their lord may not battle,
the freeman but lashes the faulty;
with Wotan's might
I should worthily war;
but Siegmund as vassal I seize.

(*Wotan turns gloomily away.*)

Who, life and body,
lies at thy bidding,
thy worshipped wife
wilt thou bend to his will?
Shall I be left
in shame to his laughter,
a spur to the bold,
a spoil for the bad?
So will my husband not have it,
my godhood more safely he guards!

WOTAN
(*gloomily*).
Say, what seek'st thou?

FRICKA.
Give from the Wolsung!

WOTAN
(*with muffled voice*).
His way let him go.

FRICKA.
But thou—shelter him not,
when vengeance shouts on his name.

WOTAN.
I—shelter him not.
FRICKA.
Lean not on falsehood,
look in my face!
The Walkyrie turn from him too!
WOTAN.
The Walkyrie freely fare!
FRICKA.
Nowise! To thy will
she is bound in her work;
forbid her from Siegmund's side!
WOTAN
(with violent inward struggle).
I never can slay him;
he found my sword!
FRICKA.
Unhallow the weapon,
or hurl it in halves!
Fenceless behold him the foe!
(*She hears from the height Brünnhilde's joyous Walkyrie-cry, who appears at this moment on the rocky path to the right.*)
To meet thee thy hardy maid
hither comes with her cry.
WOTAN
(hollowly to himself).
I had her for Siegmund to horse!
FRICKA.
Of thy holy wife's
unheeded worship
be shelter here her shield!
With laughter of men
and loss of our might,
low would our godhood be gone,
were not high to-day
and wholly my due
upheld by thy mettlesome maid.

The Wolsung's end is my welfare;
betides me from Wotan the oath?

WOTAN.
(*in terrible dejection and inward rage throwing himself upon a seat of rock*).
Take the oath!

(*As Brünnhilde from the height caught sight of Fricka she suddenly ceased her song, and has now led her horse by the bridle quietly and slowly down the rock; she is hiding him in a cave, as Fricka, turning back to her chariot, passes by her.*)

FRICKA
(*to Brünnhilde*).
War-father,
for thee waits;
from him thou learnest
how he has chosen the lot!

(*She mounts the chariot and drives quickly away to the background.*)

BRÜNNHILDE
(*walks with wondering and anxious air to Wotan, who, leaning back on the rocky seat with his head on his hand, is sunk in gloomy thought*).
Ill fear I
ends the fight,
the lot is laughter for Fricka!—
Father, what has
thy child to hear of?
Wild I behold thee and wistful!

WOTAN
(*lets his arm drop powerlessly and his head sink in his bosom*).
My own fetter
on me falls;
all are freer than I am!

BRÜNNHILDE.
What sickens thy heart?
When saw I thee so?

WOTAN
(*lifting his arm in wild outbreak*).
O holiest shame!
O hatefullest harm!

Gods'-need!
Gods'-need!
Unending rage!
Unresting ill!
No sorrow like mine can be suffered!

BRÜNNHILDE
(*in alarm drops her spear and helmet, and with loving solicitude sinks at Wotan's feet*).
Father! Father!
What has befallen?
How thou chillest with terror thy child!
With trust in me,
O meet my truth;
see, Brünnhild' beseeches!
(*She lays affectionately and anxiously her head and hands upon his knees and bosom.*)

WOTAN
(*looks long into her eyes and then strokes her hair; as if coming to himself out of deep thought, he begins at length with very low voice*).
Were I to speak it,
would it not spoil
the hasping hold of my will?

BRÜNNHILDE
(*answering him in equally low tones*).
To Wotan's will thou talkest,
tellest thou me of thy mind;
what would she be,
were not Brünnhild' thy will?

WOTAN.
What none may in words from me witness,
by name be always
out of knowledge;
the ear thou hear'st with
is but my own.—
(*With voice still more suppressed and shy, while he looks unalteringly into Brünnhilde's eyes.*)
When love its young
delight had allayed,
I longed in my mind for might,

and worked, in reinless
reach of my will,
to win myself the world.
  Witlessly trod I
  ways of untrueness,
  hallowed by bargains
  what hid a harm;
lied and misled me had Loge,
who soon from sight I lost.
  But from love myself
  not long I could sever;
in my might I moved to its sweetness;
  the son of night,
  the secret Nibelung,
Alberich, swerved from its sway;
  he cursed upon love
  and caught by his curse
the glancing gold of the Rhine,
and reached to measureless might.
  The ring that he wrought
  I craftily wrested;
  but back to the Rhine
  I bade it not roll;
  with it I paid
  for the walls of Walhall,
the bulwark that giants had built me,
from which I now bridled the world.
  Who weens of all
  that ever was—
  Erda, the wise
  unwearying Wala,
reined me away from the ring,
warned me of fall without fathom.
  Of her mind to unseal me
  more I besought her,
but wordlessly went she from sight.
Then my mood in its mirth misgave;
to know was the need of the god;
  to the womb of the world
  led me my way,

with spell of love
   to the Wala I sped,
wildered her wisdom's pride,
till she paid with words my prayer.
Knowledge she helped me with now;
a pledge I planted in her;
the wisest woman that breathes,
to Wotan Brünnhilde bore.
   With eight sisters
   I reared thee, and sought
   in you Walkyries
   ways to foil
   what the Wala unfolded
   there was to fear—
a fall unbefitting to Walhall.
   That strong for strife
   might find us the foe,
heroes I bade you to bring me.
   Whom under our harness
   we always had hampered,
   the men in whose hearts
   we had hindered the might,
   whom in treacherous bargains'
   bands we had tangled,
   abated and filled
   with fettering blindness,
   you now were to sting
   to noise and to struggle,
   their strength feed
   with unstinting fight,
that troops of trusty warmen
might hail me in Walhall's hall.
      BRÜNNHILDE.
Thy behest left we unheeded?
Many to meet thee I've led.
   What saddens thee since
   we have worked for thee so?
         WOTAN.
   A further fear;

follow me well,—
the Wala gave me its ground !
From Alberich's host
the end overhangs us ;
in hate without name
holds me the Niblung ;
I heed him not now
with his night and his numbers—
by my heroes safe I were held.
But if once the ring
again were to reach him
would Walhall's walls be unrooted ;
he who cursed at love—
and he alone—
helped by runes
of the ring, would wreak
an unending harm
on all that is high ;
the heroes' hearts
from me he would haste ;
my host he would force
to help him in fight,
and 'mid their strength
at me he would strive.
Restlessly set I myself
to fence the ring from his finger ;
the last alive
of the giants whose labour
with woeful gold
I guerdoned once,
Fafner, broods on the wealth
he felled his brother to win.
My need was again to get
from him now the meed I had given ;
but my hand from its blow
is held by my bargain ;
mightless with him
my mettle it makes.
Such are the bands
that belt and swathe me ;

born was of bargains my strength,
but to bargains still I must bend.
　To work what foils me
　befits but one,
　a hero whose head
　I never have hallowed;
　who, far from the god
　and free from his gift,
　blindly might,
　unbidden by me,
　for need alone
　and with means he knew,
　further the deed
　I must leave undone,
that not my word had named,
though nearest it was to my wish.
　Who, in strife against
　my godhood steads me,
　so friendly a foe
　O where shall I find,
　how shape him, without
　my shelter on him,
　in his dauntless dealing
　unmeasuredly dear,
　how make him other
　than all I am,
　to work with his might
　what I may but will?
　O shame for a god!
　O shelterless grief!
　I see to sickness
　always myself
at last wherever I labour!
I waste for what shall be other—
no way what is other I win—
unfetter himself must the free-man—
slaves are the best I can breed!
　　　BRÜNNHILDE.
　But the Wolsung, Siegmund,
　works of himself!

WOTAN.
Wildly swept I
   the woods beside him;
boldly against the gods'
counsel kindled his bent—
now from their hate to save him,
nothing he has but the sword
      he lit on by gift
      and love of a god.
      Myself to catch,
      has served me my cunning!
      How lightly unfolded
      Fricka the lie!
      To farthest shame
      she fathomed my soul,
and her will to work I must suffer!

BRÜNNHILDE.
No longer is Siegmund's the lot?

WOTAN
(breaking out in wild pain of despair).
I had hands on Alberich's ring—
ran with greed at the gold!
      The curse, that I fled from,
      fast to me clings;—
what I love must so be forsaken,
murdered what most I lean on,
      met with betrayal
      his trust in me!
      Mock me no more then,
      masterful might,
      worship, and godhood's
      glittering woe!
      Asunder break
      the bulwark I set!
Here done is my work;
my hopes are dwindled to one—
      the end—
      the end!
         (He pauses in thought.)

And on the end
is bent Alberich!
Through now I fathom
the thickest thought
and wildest word of the Wala :—
" When the lightless foe of love
fiercely sows for a son,
　　the fall of the gods
　　will fast begin!"
The Niblung lately
I learned of in news
that the dwarf had worsted a woman,
whose gift was due to his gold.
　　The load of hate
　　hides in her lap,
　　the will of spite
　　spreads in her womb;
　　the wonder was left
　　the loveless workman;
but the god, who wooed as he wanted,
has never begotten his need!
　　　(With rage.)
　　So swallow my blessing,
　　Nibelung-son!
　　What goads me to sickness
　　I give thee to seize on—
my godhood's shadowy show,
to grind in thy hunger and hate!

　　　　BRÜNNHILDE
　　　　　(in alarm).
　　What charge hast thou
　　at hand for thy child?

　　　　　WOTAN
　　　　　(bitterly).
Fight wisely for Fricka,
aid for her wedlock and oath!
　　The choice she made
　　is master of mine;
what might is in Wotan's wishes?

What is free my will cannot fashion—
for Fricka's bondman
battle thy best!

BRÜNNHILDE.

Woe! Begone
from the word again!
Thou lov'st Siegmund;
thy soul's delight
I lead to, ward I the Wolsung.

WOTAN.

Siegmund hast thou to slaughter,
and Hunding befriend in the fight!
See to thyself,
be steadfast and swift;
make of thy boldness,
to meet him, the most;
a sure sword
swings Siegmund—
seek not for fear in his face!

BRÜNNHILDE.

Whom thou hast led me
wholly to love,
whom thy heart so dearly
for dauntlessness hallowed—
against him shall wield me never
thy wildering word.

WOTAN.

Ha! darest thou?
Holds thee no dread?
What art thou else than the blindly
bending way of my will?
Through my freedom with thee
waned I so far
as to seem no more
than a mock for my slaves?
Reck'st thou, child, of my wrath?

Bethink what it were,
if once my thunder
should fall thy way with its flash !
   I wrap within
   my bosom the rage
   that to terror and waste
   tosses a world
that laughed to me once for delight—
woe to him that it hits !
Scath he wins for his scorn !
   So heed me now,
   hinder me not,
but do the deed of my will ;—
   slaughter Siegmund !
Such be the Walkyrie's work !

(*He storms forth and disappears among the rocks on the left.*)

BRÜNNHILDE
(*remains a long time stupefied and frightened*).
   When saw I
   War-father so,
though strife ere here his heart has stirred ?

(*She stoops down troubled and takes up her weapons, with which she arms herself again.*)

   Why should bow me
   my weapons' weight ?
   With my heart in the fray,
   it hardly were felt !
   The fight is foul
I seek with feet so slow !

(*She considers, and then sighs.*)
   Woe, my Wolsung !
   In sorest want
must my trueness untruly forsake thee !

(*She turns towards the background and perceives Siegmund and Sieglinde, as they mount from the ravine : for a moment she observes them, as they approach, and then turns into the cavern to her horse, so that she is completely hidden from the spectators' sight.*)

(*Siegmund and Sieglinde enter. She goes hurriedly in front; he is trying to restrain her.*)

SIEGMUND.
Hold from thy haste;
rest thyself here!

SIEGLINDE.
Further! Further!

SIEGMUND
(*holds her with gentle force*).
Not further now!
Thou sweetest woman, await!
From love's most swooning
delight thou wert swept,
with reckless speed
thou sprang'st from my reach,
I hardly have reined thee here;
by wood and field,
over waste and way,
with lips of dumbness,
drov'st thou along;
no word to stay thee had weight.
(*She stares wildly before her.*)
Wait now awhile;
speak to me once—
finish this speechless fear!
See, thy brother
seizes his bride;
on Siegmund's breast thou art safe!
(*He has without her notice led her to the rocky seat.*)

SIEGLINDE
(*looks with growing transport into Siegmund's face; then passionately embraces his neck. At length she starts up with sudden terror, while Siegmund hastily seizes her*).
Away! Away!
Fly from the foulness!
Unholily
holds thee my arm!

Unblessed for bridal
my body must be;
death becomes it,
dread thou the corpse!
The wind whirl it afar,
that fixed its untruth on the true!—
While he was holding her fast,
while happy delight she found,
while wholly loved her the man,
who wholly had moved her to love,—
in her gladness's highest
holiest glimpses,
that passed her senses
and pierced to her soul,—
horror and shame
of unhallowing shackles
went like a flame
through the warrantless woman
whom long a husband had held,
whose wife she was without love!
Count her as cursed,
hold her not close!
The bearer am I
of boundless blame!
Thy faultless manhood
I must not follow;
unmeet is thy light
for me to be left in;
shame I shed on my brother,
his bridal friendship I foul!

SIEGMUND.

What shame reached thee I shall
with blood of the wronger blot!
So hasten no farther;
hold till he find us;
here—falls he before me:
if Nothung now
but gnaws his heart,
vengeance was hailed not in vain!

SIEGLINDE
(starts up and listens).
Horns! and hearken—
shouts I can hear!
Screams the risen
wrath to the sky;
aloud it yonder
yells in the land.
Hunding has slackened
his heedless sleep;
kindred and hounds
he calls on to help him;
heartily pricked
howls the pack
and barks high into heaven
over wedlock's wasted bond!
(She laughs as if beside herself; then shrinks with terror.)
Where stay'st thou, Siegmund?
See I thee still?
Burningly loved
and lightening brother!
Let thy glance's star
still again on me linger;
keep not away
from the worthless woman's kiss!—
Hark! O hark!
It is Hunding's horn!
And his pack with mouths
of murder pants.
No sword daunts
his besetting dogs;—
fling it forth, Siegmund!
Siegmund,—where art thou?
Ha, so—I see it all—
and sears me the sight!—
Hounds are flashing
their fangs for thy flesh;
light they make
of thy lordly mien;

by the feet they take thee
with fastening teeth—
thou fall'st—
asunder is sent the sword;—
what strikes the ash?
Why sinks the stem?—
Brother! My brother!
Siegmund—ha!—
(With a cry she sinks fainting into Siegmund's arms.)

SIEGMUND.
Sister! Beloved!

(He listens for her breath and convinces himself that she is still alive. He lets her slip downwards—so that, as he now himself sits down, she rests with her head on his lap. In this position they both remain till the end of the following scene.)

(A long silence during which Siegmund with tender anxiety bends over Sieglinde and plants a long kiss on her forehead.)

(Brünnhilde, leading her horse by the bridle, has slowly and solemnly walked forward out of the cave and stands now at a little distance aside from Siegmund. She carries her shield and spear in one hand, leans with the other on her horse's neck, and thus, in earnest silence, for some time watches Siegmund.)

BRÜNNHILDE.
Siegmund!
See'st thou me?
I—lead thee
hence ere long.

SIEGMUND
(raises his look to her).
Who fronts me, say,
with so sweet and smileless a face?

BRÜNNHILDE.
Whom death has hailed
as his I draw to;
who beholds my look,
he hastes from the light of life.
Where awaits him the fight
I find the warman;
who meets with me,
to fall fixed him my mind.

SIEGMUND
(*looks her long in the face, then drops his head in thought, and at last with solemn earnestness turns again to her*).

Where leav'st thou at last
the hero whom hence thou leadest?

BRÜNNHILDE.

To Walfather,
who for thee waits,
I fetch thee away;
to Walhall follow me!

SIEGMUND.

In Walhall's light
Walfather find I alone?

BRÜNNHILDE.

The fallen heroes'
friendly hands
will hold thee long
with high greeting and love.

SIEGMUND.

Find I in Walhall
Wälse, the Wolsung's father?

BRÜNNHILDE.

His father's face
shall the Wolsung find.

SIEGMUND.

Greets me a woman
gladly as well?

BRÜNNHILDE.

Wish-maidens
wait in the midst;
Wotan's daughter
deals thee sweetly the drink.

SIEGMUND.
High art thou;
holy I own thee,
O Wotan's-child;
but truth I charge thee tell me!
The bride and the sister
will be with the brother?
To clasp Siegmund
will Sieglinde come?

BRÜNNHILDE.
Life of earth
she is not loosed from;
Sieglind' not there
Siegmund will see!

SIEGMUND.
So—greet for me Walhall,
greet for me Wotan,
hail for me Wälse
and all the heroes—
hail too the matchless
fresh wish-maidens—
for now I follow thee not.

BRÜNNHILDE.
Who gazed on the Walkyrie's
withering glance,
with her has he to go!

SIEGMUND.
Where Sieglind', for bliss
or sorrow abides,
bound is Siegmund beside her;
thy look has not put
my face to paleness;
it pulls me not from the place!

BRÜNNHILDE.
With life in thy limbs
at force thou may'st laugh;

who fights with death is a fool;
for him to claim thee
came I here.

SIEGMUND.

What hero to-day
shall hew me down?

BRÜNNHILDE.

Hunding fells thee in fight.

SIEGMUND.

With death from him
thou wilt hardly daunt me;
cam'st thou in hope
here of a corpse,
his it fits thee to have;
for whole is my faith in his fall.

BRÜNNHILDE
(shaking her head).

Thine, Wolsung,
thus thou art warned—
thine was at last the lot.

SIEGMUND.

See'st thou this sword?
Who sent it me,
he made me safe;
I think no more of thy threats!

BRÜNNHILDE
(strongly raising her voice).

Who dealt thee the sword,
now seeks he thy death—
and the spell he lent it is sped!

SIEGMUND
(impetuously).

Soft, and wreck not
the slumberer's rest!

(He bends, with an outburst of grief, tenderly over Sieglinde.)

Woe ! Woe !
Thou sweetest at once
and saddest and surest of women !
In weapons against thee
gathers the world,
and he who alone is thy stay,
for whom thou withstood'st it alone—
with all its shield
shall his arm not shade thee,—
forsake thee so far in the fight ?—
Ha ! shame to him,
who behind his sword,
so dooms me, for victory, death !
Fall if he makes me,
I fare not to Walhall—
Hella fetter me fast !

    BRÜNNHILDE
     (moved).
So worthless deem'st thou
undying welfare ?
Nought is thy want
but the woman now,
whose failing weight
so faintly lies in thy lap ?
Thou yearnest nowhere beyond ?

    SIEGMUND
  (bitterly looking up to her).
How sweet and young
thou seemest to sight ;
but cold and hard
calls thee my heart !
Would'st thou but mock me,
move on thy way,
thou mean, unwomanly maid !
But must thou be witness
to woe of mine,
my harm shall gladden thee here,
and my grief shall heal
the greed of thy heart :—

but on Walhall's chary blisses
I charge thee waste not a breath!

   BRÜNNHILDE
   (*with increasing interest*).
The need I behold
that gnaws at thy heart!
I feel for the hero's
holiest fear—
Siegmund, thy wife to me leave;
she safe shall live at my side!

   SIEGMUND.
No other than I
in her life shall ever uplift her;
 if fixed is my fall,
I shall slay her first in her sleep!

   BRÜNNHILDE.
Wolsung! Hark to me!
Wild are thy words;
to save her I plead
for the pledge's sake
that so sweetly with her thou hast placed!

   SIEGMUND
   (*drawing his sword*).
This sword—
that was truthlessly sent to the true—
this sword—
that forsakes me in face of the foe—
help if it fails in with him—
befriends me with her to the full!

   (*Pointing the sword at Sieglinde.*)
Two lives
with a laugh to thee turn;—
strike them, Nothung,
hungering steel!
Bite, with a stroke, at both!

BRÜNNHILDE
(in an impetuous storm of sympathy).
Withhold, Wolsung,
hark to my word !
Sieglind' shall live—
and Siegmund leave her not lone !
My mind is made !
The lots I master—
so for Siegmund
blessing and battle I save.
(The sound of horns is heard from the distant background.)
Hear'st thou his horn ?
The foe is at hand !
Trust, as thou swingest
the sword, in its truth ;
staunch is the steel in thy grasp,
and the Walkyrie guards thee well ;
so hail, Siegmund,
happiest hero !
At the fight I shall further behold thee !
(She storms away and disappears with her horse in a side-hollow to the right. Siegmund, joyful and uplifted, looks after her.)
(The stage has gradually become dark ; heavy storm-clouds sink down over the background and gradually and completely veil the walls of rock, the ravine, and the high ridge. From the distance on all sides is heard the cry of trumpets, which, during what follows, sound gradually nearer.)

SIEGMUND
(bending over Sieglinde).
Sleep its spell
has sweetly spread,
her heart to soothe from harm ;
when the Walkyrie came to my side,
was the kindly slumber her work ?
Deemed she the whirl of the swords
a suffering woman would daunt ?
Lifeless looks she,
and yet she lives ;
a laughing dream
has lightened her dread.—
(Fresh trumpet-cries.)

K

Be sound in thy sleep,
till the fight be past
and peace thou wake to find!

(*He lays her softly on the rocky bank, kisses her brow, and then, after repeated trumpet-cries, goes off.*)

Who warns me so loud,
let him beware;
here shall he draw
wholly his due;
Nothung's now is the debt!

(*He hastens towards the background, and at once disappears on the ridge in the dark storm-cloud.*)

SIEGLINDE
(*dreaming*).

But that my father were back!
In the forest he fares with the boy.
Mother! Mother!
My heart's amiss;—
not mild and still
is the strangers' meaning!—
Blasts of blackness—
smothering smoke—
fiery tongues
and fingers I feel—
the building burns—
be with me, brother!
Siegmund! Help me!

(*Strong lightnings flash through the clouds; a terrible thunder-clap wakes Sieglinde; she starts suddenly up.*)

Siegmund! Ha!

(*She stares round her with increasing fear; nearly the whole stage is veiled with black storm-clouds; continued lightning and thunder. From all sides the horns sound nearer and nearer.*)

HUNDING'S
(*voice in the background—from the ridge*).

Wehwalt! Wehwalt!
Stay for my stroke!
Stand, or my hounds shall withhold thee!

SIEGMUND'S
(voice from further in the background—out of the ravine).
Where hast thou hid,
that I left thee behind?
Rest, and let me reach thee!

SIEGLINDE
(who listens in terrible agitation).
Hunding—Siegmund—
here I should see them!

HUNDING'S
(voice).
Enough, thou warrantless wooer;
Fricka finish thee now!

SIEGMUND'S
(voice now also on the ridge).
Still counts me unweaponed
thy coward's wit?
Fright me with women—
but fight as well—
or Fricka leaves thee unfenced!
Behold; from the steadfast
stem of thy house
unsheathed I strongly the sword
with its blade to strike for thy blood!

(A flash for a moment lightens the ridge on which Hunding and Siegmund are now seen fighting.)

SIEGLINDE
(with all her strength).
You men! No further!
Murder me first!

(She rushes towards the ridge; a bright light, breaking from the right over the fighters, suddenly dazzles her so strongly that she turns aside as if blinded. In the light Brünnhilde appears floating over Siegmund and covering him with her shield.)

BRÜNNHILDE'S
(voice).
Wound him, Siegmund!
Safe is the weapon!

(As Siegmund is lifting his arm for a deadly stroke at Hunding, a glowing red light breaks from the left through the clouds, in which Wotan appears standing over Hunding and stretching his spear across against Siegmund.)

WOTAN'S
(voice).
Sink from the shaft!
In shivers the sword!

(Brünnhilde, in terror, has fallen back before Wotan with her shield; Siegmund's sword breaks on the outstretched spear; Hunding drives his sword into his undefended breast. Siegmund falls to the ground. Sieglinde, who hears his last breath, with a shriek drops as if lifeless to the earth.)
(With Siegmund's fall the light on both sides has disappeared; thick darkness lies in the clouds up to the front; in it Brünnhilde is indistinctly seen as, in sudden haste, she turns to Sieglinde.)

BRÜNNHILDE.
To horse, that safe I may have thee!

She catches Sieglinde up to her on her horse that is standing close to the side-hollow, and immediately disappears with her.)
(The clouds are at once divided in the middle, so that Hunding is clearly seen drawing his sword out of the fallen Siegmund's breast. Wotan, surrounded with cloud, stands behind him upon a rock, leaning upon his spear and painfully gazing at Siegmund's body.)

WOTAN
(after a short silence, turned towards Hunding).
Afar, slave!
Fall before Fricka;
speak that by Wotan's spear
is well her vengeance worked.—
Go!—Go!—

(At the contemptuous wave of his hand Hunding sinks dead to the ground.)

WOTAN
(suddenly breaking out in terrible anger).
But—Brünnhilde!
Woe to her wickedness!
Fearful be
the boon of her fault,
or fail my horse of her flight!

(He disappears with lightning and thunder. The curtain falls quickly.)

THIRD ACT.

On the top of a rocky height. (On the right a fir-wood bounds the scene. On the left the entrance to a rocky cavern, which forms a natural hall; above it the rock climbs to its highest point. Towards the back the prospect is quite open; rocks of greater and less height form the border of the precipice, which—as is to be assumed—slopes steeply down to the background. Detached clouds, as if driven by a storm, sweep past the rocky edge.)
(The names of the eight Walkyries who—beside Brünnhilde—appear in this scene, are: Gerhilde, Ortlinde, Waltraute, Schwertleite, Helmwige, Siegrune, Grimgerde, Rossweisse.)
(Gerhilde, Ortlinde, Waltraute, and Schwertleite are stationed on the point of rock at and over the cavern; they are in full armour.)

GERHILDE
(highest of all and turned towards the background).
Hoyotoho! Hoyotoho!
Heiaha! Heiaha!
Helmwige, here!
Hither thy horse!
(The gleam of lightning breaks out in a passing cloud; a Walkyrie on horseback appears in it; over her saddle hangs a slain warrior.)

HELMWIGE'S
(voice from without).
Hoyotoho! Hoyotoho!

ORTLINDE, WALTRAUTE, AND SCHWERTLEITE
(calling to her as she approaches).
Heiaha! Heiaha!
(The cloud with the Walkyrie's appearance has vanished behind the wood on the right.)

ORTLINDE
(calling into the wood).
By Ortlinde's filly
fasten him up;
graze shall my Gray
and thy Bay there together!

WALTRAUTE
(in like manner).
Who hangs at thy saddle?

HELMWIGE
(coming out of the wood).
Sintolt the Hegeling!

SCHWERTLEITE.
Forth with the Bay,
and bind him afar!
Ortlinde's warman
is Wittig the Irming!

GERHILDE
(has come down a little nearer).
Unfailing foes
they always were found!

ORTLINDE
(starts up and runs into the wood).
With his heels at my filly
too fierce is thy horse!

SCHWERTLEITE AND GERHILDE
(laugh aloud).
The heroes left
their hate to the horses!

HELMWIGE
(calling back into the wood).
Steady my Bay, there!
Stir not the stable!

WALTRAUTE
(on the look-out in Gerhilde's place at the highest point).
Hoyotoho! Hoyotoho!
Heiaha! Heiaha!
Siegrune, here!
What hindered thee so?

(Siegrune, in the same manner as Helmwige before, passes by to the wood.)

SIEGRUNE'S
(voice from the right).
Work was rife!
But await me the rest?

THE WALKYRIES.

Hoyotoho ! Hoyotoho !
Heiaha ! Heiaha !

(*Siegrune has disappeared behind the wood. From the depth are heard two voices together.*)

GRIMGERDE AND ROSSWEISSE
(from below).

Hoyotoho ! Hoyotoho !
Heiaha ! Heiaha !

WALTRAUTE.

Grimgerd' and Rossweisse !

GERHILDE.

Together they ride.

(*Ortlinde has come out of the wood with Helmwige and Siegrune who has just arrived; all three beckon downwards from the edge of the rock behind.*)

ORTLINDE, HELMWIGE, AND SIEGRUNE.

Be greeted, you gallopers !
Rossweiss' and Grimgerde !

ALL THE OTHER WALKYRIES.

Hoyotoho ! Hoyotoho !
Heiaha ! Heiaha !

(*In a cloud gleaming with lightning, which comes up from below and disappears behind the wood, are seen Grimgerde and Rossweisse also on horseback and each with a slain warrior over her saddle.*)

GERHILDE.

To wood with the runners
for bait and rest !

ORTLINDE
(calling into the wood).

Farther set
the fillies asunder,
until our heroes'
hatred is tamed !

GERHILDE
(while the others laugh).
The heroes' grudge
was hard on the Gray!
(Grimgerde and Rossweisse enter from the wood.)

THE WALKYRIES.
Welcome! Welcome!

SCHWERTLEITE.
Kept you coupled your way?

GRIMGERDE.
No mate we dreamed of,
we met but to-day.

ROSSWEISSE.
If all have alighted,
why linger we idle?
For Walhall quickly we'll make,
Wotan with quarry to meet!

HELMWIGE.
Eight are we only,
wanting is one.

GERHILDE.
With the whiling Wolsung
Brünnhild' has waited.

WALTRAUTE.
Till her we have greeted,
go we not hence;
fierce would Walfather's
welcome be found,
hailed we his face without her!

SIEGRUNE
(on the point of rock whence she is looking out).
Hoyotoho! Hoyotoho!
Behold! Behold!
At lightning speed
spurs Brünnhild' along.

THE WALKYRIES
(hurrying to the rock-point).
Heiaha! Heiaha!
Brünnhilde! Hey!

WALTRAUTE.

To the wood she steers
her staggering horse.

GRIMGERDE.

How Grane groans
with the reckless ride!

ROSSWEISSE.

So wild never
was Walkyrie's wayfare!

ORTLINDE.

What sits at her saddle?

HELMWIGE.

No hero it seems!

SIEGRUNE.

With a woman she hies!

GERHILDE.

How happed she on her?

SCHWERTLEITE.

No greeting sound
gives she her sisters!

WALTRAUTE.

Heiaha! Brünnhilde!
Hear'st thou no bit?

ORTLINDE.

Lend her a hand
as she leaps from horseback!
(Gerhilde and Helmwige hurry into the wood.)

ROSSWEISSE.

To ground the steadfast
Grane stumbles!
(*Siegrune and Waltraute follow the other two.*)

GRIMGERDE.

From the saddle wildly
swings she the woman.

THE OTHER WALKYRIES
(*hastening to the wood*).
Sister! Sister!
Why is it so?
(*All the Walkyries return to the stage; with them comes Brünnhilde
supporting and leading in Sieglinde.*)

BRÜNNHILDE
(*breathless*).
Save me, and help
in sorest harm!

THE WALKYRIES.

From whence art thou here
in wildering haste?
A fit so headlong is flight!

BRÜNNHILDE.

I fly, who had never
ere now to flee!
War-father follows my wake!

THE WALKYRIES
(*in great alarm*).
Safe are thy senses?
Speak to us! Say!
Behind is War-father?
Hunts he thy heels?

BRÜNNHILDE
(*anxiously*).
O sisters, look
from the soaring ledge!

Watch to northwards
if Walfather nears!
(*Ortlinde and Waltraute spring higher up to look out.*)
Say, is he in sight?

ORTLINDE.
A storm of thunder
from northward steers.

WALTRAUTE.
Steeply aloft
its clouds are stowed.

THE WALKYRIES.
War-father hies
on his holy horse!

BRÜNNHILDE.
The raging hunter
behind me who rides,
he nears, he nears from north!
Save me, sisters!
Ward this woman!

THE WALKYRIES.
What woman behold we?

BRÜNNHILDE.
Hear me in hurry!
Sieglind' I bring—
Siegmund's sister and bride;
down on the Wolsungs
has Wotan driven his whip;—
the brother bid he
Brünnhild' to-day
forsake to his death;
but Siegmund sheltered
she with her shield,
in spite of the god,
who galled him instead with his spear.

Siegmund fell;
but I flew
with the woman far;
her to save
I hither have swept;
and it seemed beside
your help might sway his hate from my
    head.

>   THE WALKYRIES
>   (*in the greatest consternation*).

Unguided sister!
Forgot'st thou so?
Sorrow! Sorrow!
Brünnhilde, sorrow!
Unbehoveful
held Brünnhilde
War-father's holy behest?

>   WALTRAUTE
>   (*from the height*).

Nearer draws it
like night from the north.

>   ORTLINDE
>   (*in like manner*).

Hither streams
unhindered the storm.

>   THE WALKYRIES
>   (*turned towards the background*).

Wildly whinnies
Walfather's horse,
snorts and snuffs with his heat!

>   BRÜNNHILDE.

Harm to the woman,
when Wotan is here;
he wars with unflinching
flame at the Wolsungs.—
Will none of you help
me now with a horse,
to have her widely away?

THE WALKYRIES.

Shall we fall
from our father as well?

BRÜNNHILDE.

Rossweisse, sister!
Lend me thy runner!

ROSSWEISSE.

From Walfather never
in flight he was known.

BRÜNNHILDE.

Helmwige, fail not!

HELMWIGE.

My father I follow.

BRÜNNHILDE.

Waltraute! Gerhilde!
Give me my way!
Siegrune! Ortlinde!
See me beseech!
Be true to me,
who trusted you much;
let not this woman be lost!

SIEGLINDE
(who hitherto has stared darkly and coldly before her, as Brünnhilde sharply embraces her—as if to protect her).

No sorrow shall meet thee for me;
death I dreadlessly seek!
Who bid thee bear
me here from the battle?
In storm O would I
had stayed a stroke
from the searching weapon
of Siegmund's wound,
that life no longer
than his might last!
Far from Siegmund?

Forth from his side?
In death shall the dream
of it be darkened!—
Make me not curse thee,
maid, for thy kindness—
to my prayer be holy and sweet—
plunge with thy sword to my heart!

BRÜNNHILDE.

Let not, O woman,
his love be wasted!
Live for the pledge
that he placed in thy life;
a Wolsung lies in thy womb!

SIEGLINDE
is violently startled; then suddenly her face is lighted up with lofty joy).
Bring me to shelter!
My babe for me shield!
Fold me, you maidens,
in fathomless fence!

(*A terrible storm rises in the background; approaching thunder.*)

WALTRAUTE
(*from the height*).
The storm is at hand.

ORTLINDE
(*in like manner*).
Hence ere it strike!

THE WALKYRIES.

Forth with the woman,
if Wotan she fear;
the Walkyries dare not
ward her from death!

SIEGLINDE
(*on her knees to Brünnhilde*).
Save me, O maid!
Forsake not the mother

BRÜNNHILDE
(*with quick decision*).
Away like a lightning,
O woman, alone!
I—rest to abide
the reach of his bursting wrath;
with me I hinder him
here in its might,
till safe from his search thou art made.

SIEGLINDE.
Tell me where I shall turn to!

BRÜNNHILDE.
Which of you sisters
eastward has swept?

SIEGRUNE.
Away to eastward
widens a wood,
where Fafner withholds
the Niblungs' forfeited hoard.

SCHWERTLEITE.
The shape of a worm
wears he for shelter,
and in a hole
has heed upon Alberich's hoop.

GRIMGERDE.
Not a home it were
for a helpless woman.

BRÜNNHILDE.
But round from Wotan's wrath
walls her rightly the wood;
the god mistrusts it
and treads not its ground.

WALTRAUTE
(*from the height*).
Wildly Wotan
rides to the rock.

THE WALKYRIES.
Brünnhild', the noise
of his nearness abounds!

BRÜNNHILDE
(*pointing out the way to Sieglinde*).
Off before him,
and fare to the east!
Match to thy burdens
the might of thy mood—
hunger and thirst,
hardness and thorn;
laugh—when thy need
most livingly gnaws!
For slight what now
I say to thee never;
the highest hero of earth
harbours, O woman,
thy sheltering womb!
(*She hands her the fragments of Siegmund's sword.*)
O ward for him safe
the sundered weapon;
where his father fell
I gathered it from him;
who shall grasp it whole
again in the hilt,
his name he gets from me now—
"Siegfried" of gladdening sword!

SIEGLINDE.
O mastering wonder!
Lordliest maid!
Thy truth has taught me
holiest trust!
What belongs to him
whom we loved I will harbour;
in its life at last
shall my thanks to thee laugh!
Fare thou well!
Unweariedly bless thee my woes!

(She hastens away to the right in the foreground. The height is inclosed by black storm-clouds; a terrible storm roars from the background; a fiery light brightens the fir-wood at the side. Among the thunder is heard Wotan's cry.)

WOTAN'S
(voice).
Hold! Brünnhilde!

THE WALKYRIES.

The height is reached
by horse and rider;
woe to Brünnhilde!
Wildly he burns!

BRÜNNHILDE.

Ah, sisters, help!
My heart is sick!
His rage will wreck me,
if fast you fence me not round.

THE WALKYRIES.

Hither behind us!
Come to be hid!
Cling in our midst
and meet not his call!

(They all mount the rock-point hiding Brünnhilde among them.)

Woe! Woe!
Fiercely Wotan
falls from his horse—
hither strides
the storm of his step!

(Wotan strides in terrible anger out of the wood and stops in front of the troop of Walkyries, who have taken up, on the height, such a position as protects Brünnhilde from sight.)

WOTAN.

Where is Brünnhilde,
where with her wickedness?
Seek you to hide
her sin from my summons?

THE WALKYRIES.
Fearful we deem thy fierceness;
what deed befell from thy daughters,
    that roused thee so
    to unsoftening rage?

WOTAN.
Mean you to mock me?
Bridle your boldness!
I know—Brünnhild'
you bar from me now.
Leave her from all
for ever an offcast,
as she her worth
has shorn away!

THE WALKYRIES.
She fled hither before thee,
besought at our hands to be saved;
    with fear thy heat
    has furrowed her heart.
    For our hapless sister
    here we beseech thee
to rein the sweep of thy wrath.

WOTAN.
Weak-hearted
and womanly herd!
Such fainting minds
how found you from me?
Have I made you to fare
like men to the fight,
hearts have I shaped you
so sharp and hard,
that you wildly here should howl and whine,
when I turn on a wounder of truth?
    Now feel, you whimperers,
    what was her fault,
    for whom you trickle
    so hotly your tears!

Beside her none
saw to my innermost senses ;
not one like her
watched at the well of my wishes ;
herself was she
the working womb of my will ; —
to-day the bond
of our bliss she undid,
and falsely threatened
to fight with my thought ;
my spoken behest
unhidingly spurned,
and at me, with the weapon, she made,
that by will of mine she wore !—
Hear'st thou, Brünnhilde,
whom to thy harness,
fence, and helm,
sweetness and bliss,
name and being I brought ?
Fear'st thou the sound of my summons,
and keep'st afar like a coward,
in mind to flinch from thy meed ?

BRÜNNHILDE
(*steps out from the group of Walkyries, walks with submissive but firm tread down from the rock-point and so approaches to within a short distance from Wotan's face*).

Behold me, Father ;
my fate I am here for !

WOTAN.

From me—falls it not first ;
on thyself thy meed thou hast sent.—
My will alone
awakened thy life,
and against it lo thou hast gone ;
nought but my word
was known in thy work,
and against it warning thou givest ;
wish-maid
wert thou to me,
and against my mind thou hast warred ;

        shield-maiden
        I made thee to me,
and against me thy shield thou hast moved;
        lot-chooser
        I let thee be,
and against me the lots thou hast lifted;
        hero-stirrer
        I had thee hailed,
and against me heroes thou goadest.—
        What once thou wert,
        unfolds to thee Wotan;
        what now thou seemest,
        name to thyself!
Wish-maid art thou no more;
Walkyrie's ways thou hast ended;—
        from henceward be
        what here thou abid'st!

            BRÜNNHILDE
            (*terror-stricken*).
        Am I thrust from thee so?
        Can such be thy thought?

            WOTAN.
No more from Walhall I send thee,
        I show thee no more
        the men to be slain;
        no heroes thou guidest
        again to my hall;
where the gods at feast-time are friendly,
        the drink-horn may'st thou
        deal me no more;
        no more for my kiss
        on thy mouth thou wilt come.
        From midst of the gods
        thou art moved and forgotten,
        struck and strewn
from life on their lasting stem;
        for broken is all our bond;
out of my sight thou for ever art sent!

The Walkyries
(breaking out in distress).
Woe ! Woe !
Sister ! O sister !

Brünnhilde.
All must thou take
that thou taught'st me to own ?

Wotan.
To thy master must it be lost !
  Alone on the height
  I leave thee to lie;
  in shelterless sleep
  shalt thou be shut,
till falls the maid to the man,
who shall find her and wake by the way.

The Walkyries.
  Befits it, Father,
  to curse her so far ?
  Shall the maiden whiten
  and waste with a man ?
  O shed not so dreadful
  a shame on her deed ;
in the stain that strikes her we share !

Wotan.
  Heard you not how
  her fate I have fixed ?
  Far from your side
shall the faithless sister be sundered ;
  her horse no more
in your midst through the breezes shall haste
      her ;
  her flower of maidhood
  will falter and fade ;
  a husband will win
  her womanly heart,

she meekly will bend
to the mastering man,
the hearth she'll heed, as she spins
and to laughers is left for their sport.

(*Brünnhilde sinks with a cry at his feet; the Walkyries make a movement of horror.*)

Fear you her doom?
Then forth from her downfall!
Make from her side,
and see her no more!
Were there to linger
one with her longer—
hope to withstand me
and stay by her here,
the fool should share in the fate
I warn you wisely to shun!—
So sweep from the rock!
Swiftly bereave it!
Nimbly hence on your horses,
or await nothing but woe!

(*The Walkyries start asunder with wild cries of distress, and rush with hurried flight into the wood; soon they are heard going off like a storm on their horses. During what follows the storm gradually ceases; the clouds part; twilight and then night sink down amid calm weather.*)

(*Wotan and Brünnhilde, who still lies stretched at his feet, remain alone. A long solemn silence; the position of Wotan and Brünnhilde continues unchanged.*)

BRÜNNHILDE
(*at length slowly raising her head, seeks Wotan's still averted look, and during what follows gradually lifts herself up*).

Full of so sheer
a shame was my fault,
that with a meed now so shameful it is met?
Led me so deep
below thee my deed,
that in the depth of such downfall I am left?
Fell I at once
so far from my worth,
that so unworthy of fame I am found?
O say, Father!
Search in my face;

sink from thy wrath,
soften thy rage!
Kindle to sight
the covered sin,
that with stubborn stress besets thee
to forsake thy most chosen child!

   WOTAN
   (gloomily).
Seek of thy deed—
it sweeps the dark from thy sin!

   BRÜNNHILDE.
Thine was the word
that worked on me then.

   WOTAN.
Was what I warned thee
to fight for the Wolsung?

   BRÜNNHILDE.
Thou said'st as lord
of the lots to me so.

   WOTAN.
But back again
I grasped the bidding I gave.

   BRÜNNHILDE.
When Fricka the bent
that filled thee had broken;
when sway thou gav'st to her fancy,
against thyself thou wert foe.

   WOTAN
   (bitterly).
I deemed thou hadst fathomed me fully
and wittingly worked at thy deed;
 but senseless and faint
 before thee I seemed;
so were not betrayal thy trespass,
I should rate thee unworthy my wrath!

BRÜNNHILDE.

Not wide is my wisdom;
alone I was ware
of thy love for the Wolsung;
I knew of the strife
that had stunned thee enough
to make thee of him unmindful.
The only thing
not out of thy thought
to behold was so hard
a shock to thy heart—
that Siegmund sank from thy shelter.

WOTAN.

Thou saw'st how it stood,
and still wert staunch to his side?

BRÜNNHILDE.

For thy sake I seized on
that thing with my sight,
which, in hold of the other
harassed and hurt,
thou leftest unlooked to behind thee.
Who for Wotan warded
his back in the war,
she only could see
what thou saw'st not at all;—
of nought but Siegmund I knew.
In death's name
I drew to him now,
beheld how he seemed
and heard what he said,
till I knew the hero's
holiest need;
his grief in the tongue
of a trumpet he gave me—
love in its widest
lordliest woe,
sorrow's unscanted
silencing scorn;

I beheld and heard,
while I looked and hearkened,
what shot unbarred to my breast
and holily shook me at heart.—
   Shy and startled
   stood I in shame;
   how I could help him
   haunted me wholly;
   safety or death
   with Siegmund to draw for—
   such was the lot
   that alone I could seek!
   Whose breath had lifted
   this love in my breast,
   thy will, that gave me
   the Wolsung to guard,
seemed with me for guide
against the word thou hadst said.

   WOTAN.
   So hast thou done
what to do so wholly I hoped—
   but what not to do
I now doubly was doomed?
   So light to thee seemed
sweetness of love to be lit on,
   when burning grief
   in my breast began,
   when harrowing fate
   with fierceness filled me,
   for love of a world,
   the well of love
in my wildered heart to hinder?
   When against myself
   I searingly sided,
   when from wounds of faintness
   in foam I was wasted,
   till branding wants
   and bridleless wishes
brought me the withering will,

in the wreck of my world itself,
to be rid of a slumberless sorrow,—
 alone thy food
 was laughing delight,
 for feeling's blind
 and fathomless bliss
 thy lips were deep
 in the drink of love—
while mine winced at the gall
mixed with the woefare of gods?—
 Thy fooling thought
 freely then follow;
aloof thou hast left me far.
 No more may we meet,
 nor seek to be mixed
in whispered sounds of wisdom;
 in work no further
 thou fondly art with me;
in life nowhere and light
is again the god to be near thee!

   BRÜNNHILDE.
 Thou foundest unmeet
 the foolish maid,
 who saw not for wonder
 what thou hadst said,
 while from all I had learned
 my belief was alone—
to love what thou first hadst loved.—
 Must I then leave thee
 and meet thee no longer,
 wilt thou then sunder,
 what once was the same,
 a part of thyself
 aside from thee put,
that thy own it seemed to thee always,
thou god, forget not so!
 Thy other half
 thou wilt not unhallow,
 shame wilt not wish me,
 in which thou must share;

thy own fall thou wilt look on,
if open to laughter I'm found!

WOTAN.

Thou followed'st lightly
the might of love;
now follow the man
whom love thou must!

BRÜNNHILDE.

Shall I be shut from Walhall,
from share in thy work and thy wisdom,
must I belong
to the mastering man—
a bloodless boaster
let him not be;
no worth may he,
who shall win me, want!

WOTAN.

From Walfather turned the maid—
he may not choose for her more.

BRÜNNHILDE.

Forget not the race thou begot'st,
from its root no coward can come;
the holiest hero—I know it—
from the Wolsungs' blood is at hand!

WOTAN.

Name not the Wolsungs anew!
With them I have done,
when from thee I withdraw;
and hate has hunted them down.

BRÜNNHILDE.

When I swerved from thy word,
the Wolsungs I saved;
Sieglinde holds
the holiest seed;

in need and woe
to woman unknown,
forth she will bring
what she flees with in fear.

WOTAN.

Hope not at my hand
welfare for her,
nor the fruit that fills her womb!

BRÜNNHILDE.

She has got the sword
that to Siegmund thou gav'st—

WOTAN.

And whose blade, as he swung it, I broke!
Seek not, O maid,
my mind to unsettle!
Abide the lot
to which thou art bound;
no might to bend it is mine!—
But forth I must needs
fare from thee now,
too far already I rest.
From her who turned from me
here I must turn;
I may know not what
she names in her wish;
her fate alone
I must leave fulfilled.

BRÜNNHILDE.

What seems to thee meet
for me to suffer?

WOTAN.

In steadfast sleep
I seal thee straight;
who finds thee fenceless on high,
he wakes and has thee for wife.

BRÜNNHILDE
(falls on her knees).
Ere fettering sleep
fast shall fix me
for bootless coward
as bounden booty,
a deed behold thou must do me,
the hope of holiest dread—
    the slumberer harbour
    with hindering horror,
    that none but a free
    unfaltering hero,
    here on the height
    may make me his !

WOTAN.
Too much thou graspest—
too great a meed !

BRÜNNHILDE
(embraces his knees).
The boon thou shalt—
shalt not forbear from !
Or strike at me now
as I strangle thy knee,
thy darling mangle,
to dust with thy maid,
from her body spill
the breath with thy spear ;
but not fiercely unfence
her here to a nameless harm !

(Wildly.)

O with thy word
a fire awaken,
to redden with towering
terror the rock,
with tongues to lick
and with teeth to tear
the boaster whose road may bring him
in reach of its bellowing rim !

WOTAN

(looks with emotion into her eyes and lifts her up).

Farewell, thou choice
unwavering child!
Thou holy pastime
and pride of my heart!
Farewell! Farewell! Farewell!
Must I forsake thee,
and may I sweetly
no more give thee my greeting;
must we guide not again
our horses together;
must my cup by another be handed;
after our love
O am I to leave thee,
thou laughing delight of my eyes;—
a buoyanter beacon
shall burn for thy bridal
than ever has blazed for a bride!
To fringe the rock
a flame I will raise;
with withering clasp
it shall wait for the coward;
the falterer fly
from Brünnhilde's fence!
To gain her is given but one—
who is freer than I, the god!

(Brünnhilde, with emotion and transport, throws herself into his arms.

On the lighting pair of thy eyes,—
that lay so oft at my lips,
when for flash of coming
fight I kissed them,
when in sounds of childhood
the song that cheered
the heroes swelled from thy heart;
on the steadfast pair of thy eyes,—
that so oft were stars of my storm,
when hope was fierce
in my heart like fire,

when world's-delightwards
my will was lifted
from dread wildering darkness,—
for latest healing
here I must lean
in last farewell
of lingering lips !
The happier man
to meet them be hailed !
On the luckless god
they gaze no longer to light him !
For so—goes
the god from thy side;
so weans he thy godhood away.

(*He kisses her on both eyes which immediately shut and remain closed she sinks softly, as if weary, back into his arms. He carries her and lays her tenderly on a low mound of moss over which stretches a wide-branched fir. He once more looks at her face and then shuts fast her helmet; then again his look lingers sadly on her figure, which he at last covers with the long steel shield of the Walkyrie. He then walks with solemn resolution into the middle of the stage and turns the point of his spear towards a large mass of rock.*)

Loge, hear !
Hitherward listen !
As I found thee at first—
in arrowy flame,
as thereafter thou fleddest—
in fluttering fire ;
as I dealt with thee once,
I wield thee to-day !
Arise, billowing blaze,
and fold in thy fire the rock !
Loge ! Loge ! Aloft !

(*At the last call he strikes three times with his spear on the stone, whereupon a flame starts out of it, which quickly spreads into a sea of fire, to which Wotan points out with his spear the rim of the rock for its flow.*)

Who fears the spike
of my spear to face,
he will pierce not the planted fire !

(*He disappears in the fire towards the background.*)

(*The curtain falls.*)

SECOND DAY.

SIEGFRIED.

PERSONS.

Siegfried.
Mime.
The Wanderer.
Alberich.
Fafner.
Erda.
Brünnhilde.

SIEGFRIED.

FIRST ACT.

Forest. (The foreground is formed by part of a natural cavern, which towards the left stretches deeper inwards, but towards the right occupies about three-quarters of the stage. Two naturally-formed entrances are open towards the forest; the one to the right issues immediately, the broader one sideways on to the background. Against the back-wall to the left stands a large forge naturally formed out of pieces of rock; the great bellows are all that is artificial. The rough chimney—also natural—goes up through the roof of the rock. A very large anvil and other smith's implements.)

MIME

(*as the curtain rises after a brief orchestral prelude, is sitting at the anvil and, with growing uneasiness, hammering at a sword; at length, in ill-humour, he stops his work*).

Toil without guerdon!
Wearisome task!
The fittest sword
that ever I forged,
in the fist of giants
firm it were found;
but he it was made for,
the mannerless youngster,
will smash and smite it in two,
as if I had turned out a toy!

A sword that I know
he were slow to sunder;
with Nothung's bits
he needs would forbear,
could I but splice
the cursed splinters,
that all my mind
will not aid me to mend.

Might I but weld the weapon,
I should reap a meed for my wrong!
(He sinks farther back and bends his head in thought.)
Fafner, the sullen Worm,
sits in the gloomy wood,
where he binds with his body's weight
    the Nibelung's hoard
    hidden beneath.
Fafner's body would bend
to Siegfried's boyish force;
    the Nibelung's ring
    through him I should reach.
The sword to work it is one;
and Nothung fits to my need,
when Siegfried swings him like fire;—
    but unwelded I see him,
    Nothung the sword!—
(He proceeds, in greatest ill-humour, to hammer the sword.)
Toil without guerdon!
Wearisome task!
The fittest sword,
that I ever forged,
    would never do
    for the needful deed!
I beat it and heat it but
    for the boy's behest;
he'll smash and smite it in bits,
yet blame if slumbers his smith!

(Siegfried, in wild forest clothing, with a silver horn at a chain, comes boisterously in from the wood; he has bridled a great bear with a rope, and drives it, with loud merriment, at Mime. In fright Mime lets fall the sword; he runs behind the hearth; Siegfried drives the bear after him in all directions.)

SIEGFRIED.

Hoyho! Hoyho!
At him! At him!
Eat him! Eat him!
Unsightly smith!
(He laughs immoderately.)

MIME.
Out with the beast!
Why bring me the bear?

SIEGFRIED.
I brought a neighbour,
to nudge thee the better;
Browny, see for the sword!

MIME.
Let him away!
Here lies the weapon;
rubbed and ready for work.

SIEGFRIED.
And so to-day thou art safe!
(*He loosens the bear's bridle and gives him a blow on the back with it.*)
Off, Browny;
thy business is over!
(*The bear runs back into the wood.*)

MIME
(*comes out trembling from behind the hearth*).
To kill the bears
I cannot blame thee;
why lead them home
to me here alive?

SIEGFRIED
(*seats himself to recover from his laughter*).
I hoped for a comelier comrade
than sits by my side at home;
the heart of the forest my horn
filled with a sounding signal;
 "Who will come till he finds me,
 "and call me friend?"
I freely said with its sound.

From the bushes hied a bear,
who listened and looked and howled,
and I bore him better than thee,
though better still I could stand;

but I brought him hither
bridled in hemp,
to waken thy haste with the weapon.

(He leaps up and goes towards the sword.)

MIME
(seizes the sword to hand it to Siegfried).
The sword I well have set ;
for a sharper wilt thou not wish.

SIEGFRIED
(takes the sword).
What steads me a shining weapon,
if weakness shames its steel ?

(He tests it with his hand.)

Hey ! What a trumpery
toy is here !
The sullen skewer
thou say'st is a sword ?

(He strikes it to pieces on the anvil, so that the bits fly about ; Mime frightened, gets out of the way.)

Unbounded bungler,
gather the bits ;
would I had shattered it
over thy shoulders !—
At last shall thy chatter
cheat me no longer !
Thou blab'st about giants
and blustering battles,
of manful doings
and masterly deeds ;
thou serv'st me with weapons,
swords thou weldest,
always as boundless
boastest thy art ;
and when I handle
what thou hast hammered
a grasp will dint
and grind it to dirt !—

Were not the knave
too nasty to near,
with his blades and his hilts,
I'd hammer him up,—
the old unfurthering fright!
My sickness were so at an end!

(*He throws himself in a rage on to a stone seat on the right.*)

MIME
(*who has all through kept carefully out of his way*).
Now mad thou growest again!
Such guerdon must I meet?—
Bring the unthankful boy
not the best in all he bids,
and all I gave him good
in haste his heart forgets!
When wilt thou take to thought
of the thanks I have tried to teach thee?
To him at least thou should'st listen,
whose love thou wholly hast had.

Siegfried turns ill-humouredly away, with his face to the wall, so that his back is to Mime.)

My words no further thou bearest!—
Will food more welcome be?
I'll fetch the meat from the fire;
or may I the broth not bring?
For thee yonder it brews.

(*He offers food to Siegfried, who, without turning round, knocks the pot and the meat out of his hand.*)

SIEGFRIED.
Meat I served to myself;
at thy messes lap alone!

MIME
(*pretends to be hurt*).
Such an end awaited
all my work?
Learn I this way
the wages of love?—

Mime

(*at some distance seats himself familiarly opposite him*).
A witness here thou holdest
how warmly I'm with thee at heart.

Siegfried
(*laughs*).
Thy sight is grief to suffer,—
forget not such so soon!

Mime.

With thy wildness abides the blame,—
thou should'st break thy will of its ways.—
Younglings that miss their mother
yearn for the nest they knew;
love is nothing but longing;
so when thou longest for me,
it warns thee thou lovest thy Mime—
    and love him thou must!—
What the bird to the brood it breeds
and nurses in its nest,
ere the fledgling can flutter,
such to the shoot of thy youth
is Mime's motherly shelter—
such still it must stay.

Siegfried.

Ey, Mime, art thou so clever,
a matter more thou can'st clear!

    The birds for the sweetness
    of Spring were in song,
and each was seeking the other;
    thou said'st thyself,
    when I wanted word,
the male was wooing the mother.
    He came to her softly
    and sat by her side,
    a feathery nest
    they fitted and filled;

young wings were awakened
  and waved about,
and worms were brought to the brood.—
  So dwell in the copse
  by couples the deer,
so wolves and wandering foxes;
  home with fodder
  hastens the father,
the whelps have milk from the mother;
  and here I learned
  what like is love;
  no whelps from their dam
  have I drawn away.—
  Where ownest thou, Mime,
  thy mate like the others,
for me to call her mother?

        MIME
       (*peevishly*).
What is thy whim?
Lost are thy wits?
Is a fowl thy like—or a fox?

     SIEGFRIED.
The whimpering babe
thou wistfully bred'st,
thou warm'dst with linen
the little worm;—
but why should Mime
have met with the worm?
He manfully made it
without a mate?

        MIME
   (*in great perplexity*).
What I tell
for truth must be taken;
thy father I was
and mother as well.

SIEGFRIED.

Thou false unwitting old fool!—
How whelps are their father's likeness,
is what I have luckily learned.
I bent to the shining brook,
    and beheld in it beast
    and bird and bushes;
    sun and shadows,
    faithfully shown,
before me I saw at my feet.
    My face in the midst
    I further found;
    but, Mime, thy looks
    made it no match;
    such fellow's a toad
    to a flickering fish;
but toads are not fathers of fishes!

MIME
(very irritably).

Wildering nonsense
now are thy words!

SIEGFRIED
(with increasing vivacity).

Lo of a sudden
at last I see
what has vexed me so long in vain;
    when I fly my farthest
    into the forest,
what it is that hurries me home!

(He leaps up.)

No mouth but Mime's unfolds me
what father and mother were mine!

MIME
(gets out of his way).

What father? what mother?
Fanciful folly!

SIEGFRIED
(takes him by the throat).
And so I must seize thee
to make thee say it ;
ungrudged
I shall gather not aught !
Nought without force
and fight were my knowledge ;
hardly speech
I here should have heard of,
had fright not wrung it
forth from the rogue !
Now open
thy mouth with it all ;
who are my father and mother ?

MIME
(after nodding his head and making signs with his hands, has been loosed by Siegfried).
Thou hardly leav'st me with life !—
Withhold ! Thou shalt learn, of the news
thou lackest, the whole that I know.—
    O unthankful
    and thoughtless boy !
Behold ! what brings me thy hatred !
    Call me not father
    nor furthest kin,—
yet see how thou ow'st me thyself !
    Unknown and in need,
    befriended by none,
    in freeness of heart,
    I harboured thee here ;
and mannerly meed I have found !
Like a fool I thought upon thanks !

A woman once in harm
I heard from the wildering wood ;
I fetched her fast to the hole
and filled her with heat from the hearth.

SIEGFRIED.

Thou false unwitting old fool!—
How whelps are their father's likeness,
is what I have luckily learned.
I bent to the shining brook,
    and beheld in it beast
    and bird and bushes;
    sun and shadows,
    faithfully shown,
before me I saw at my feet.
    My face in the midst
    I further found;
    but, Mime, thy looks
    made it no match;
    such fellow's a toad
    to a flickering fish;
but toads are not fathers of fishes!

MIME
(very irritably).

Wildering nonsense
now are thy words!

SIEGFRIED
(with increasing vivacity).

Lo of a sudden
at last I see
what has vexed me so long in vain;
    when I fly my farthest
    into the forest,
what it is that hurries me home!

(He leaps up.)

No mouth but Mime's unfolds me
what father and mother were mine!

MIME
(gets out of his way).

What father? what mother?
Fanciful folly!

Siegfried
(takes him by the throat).

And so I must seize thee
to make thee say it;
ungrudged
I shall gather not aught!
Nought without force
and fight were my knowledge;
hardly speech
I here should have heard of,
had fright not wrung it
forth from the rogue!
Now open
thy mouth with it all;
who are my father and mother?

Mime
(after nodding his head and making signs with his hands, has been loosed by Siegfried).

Thou hardly leav'st me with life!—
Withhold! Thou shalt learn, of the news
thou lackest, the whole that I know.—
O unthankful
and thoughtless boy!
Behold! what brings me thy hatred!
Call me not father
nor furthest kin,—
yet see how thou ow'st me thyself!
Unknown and in need,
befriended by none,
in freeness of heart,
I harboured thee here;
and mannerly meed I have found!
Like a fool I thought upon thanks!

A woman once in harm
I heard from the wildering wood;
I fetched her fast to the hole
and filled her with heat from the hearth.

A babe weighed in her womb;
sadly it broke to sight;
from side to side she wound,
with will and hand I helped;
deep was the hurt, she died—
but Siegfried—he was saved.

SIEGFRIED
(seating himself).
So died my mother by me?

MIME.

She in trust to me gave the child;
the charge I gladly took.
What labour Mime has made!
What loss by his goodness has got!
 "The whimpering babe
 "I wistfully bred" . . .

SIEGFRIED.

With such thou hast filled me before
Now say why my name is Siegfried?

MIME.

Thy mother besought
that so I should make it;
as "Siegfried" soon
thou wert fair and sound.—
"I warmed with linen
"the little worm" . . .

SIEGFRIED.

Now what was the name of my mother?

MIME.

I wear it not in mind!
 "I fed thee with meat
 "and milk to the fill". . .

SIEGFRIED.

Her name I will have from thy knowledge!

MIME.
I seem to forget !—but soft !
Sieglinde is it, who made thee
so sadly over to me ?—
    " I watched thee as well
    " as the skin I wear " . . .

SIEGFRIED.
But further, who was my father ?

MIME
(sharply).
Him I have never seen.

SIEGFRIED.
But my mother must have said it ?

MIME.
That he was slain,
was the whole that I heard ;
my breast she filled
with the fatherless babe ;—
" And when thou wert taller
" I tended thee too ;
" for smiling slumber
" thy bed I smoothed " . . .

SIEGFRIED.
Staunch thy unceasing
starling-song !—
Ere I can trust thy tidings,
if thou hast lied not wholly,
let me a sign behold.

MIME.
What weight is in such a witness ?

SIEGFRIED.
I trust no tale that is said,
I trust the sight that I see ;
what token seals thy truth ?

MIME
(after some thought fetches the two pieces of a broken sword).
Mark what thy mother gave me;
for grief and wasting worry
she made me this worthless meed.
Behold the shards of a sword!
She said thy father held it,
when in last of his fights he fell.

SIEGFRIED.
To work at once
and soundly weld it!
So win I the sword I want!
Here with it, Mime,
hasten thy hands;
smite with the meetest
might of a smith!
Trifle not now
with needy tricks;
the splinters alone
I look to for speed.
If I find thee slow,
if falsely thou fit'st
or stick'st unfairly
the flawless steel,—
I'll break thy treacherous back,
and teach thee better thy trade!
I swear thou shalt see me
swing it to-day;
the weapon I'll win before dark.

MIME
(alarmed).
What seek'st thou to do with the sword?

SIEGFRIED.
From the wood forth
in the world fare;
back no further to be!
How I freshen
in my freedom,
nothing fetters me now!

No father have I here,
and afar I find my home;
thy roof is not my house,
at thy hearth I need not rest.
  As the fish flows
  in the full flood,
  as the finch flees
  with his wings wide,
  forward I fly,
  fleetly I float,
  like wind of the wood
  whistle away—
to meet with thee, Mime, no more!
(*He darts off into the wood.*)

MIME
(*in greatest distress*).
Whither? Whither? Withhold!
(*He calls with all his might into the wood.*)
  Hi! Siegfried!
  Siegfried! Hi!—
  So hence he storms;
  and here I stay.
  On former need
  follows a fresher,
and done for behold me indeed!—
  How help myself here?
  How fix him at home?
  Whom now shall I fare with
  to Fafner's nest?—
  How strive with the splinters
  of spiteful steel?
  Not a forge whose fire
  reddens them fitly;
  not a dwarf whose hammer
  deals with their hardness;
  the Niblung's heat,
  greed and need,
serve me not Nothung to heal,
help not the sword to be whole —
(*He sinks, in despair, on to the stool behind the anvil.*)

(*The Wanderer* [*Wotan*] *enters from the wood by the hinder door of the cave. He wears a long dark-blue cloak, and carries a spear as a staff. On his head he has a large hat with broad round brim, which hangs far down over the place of his missing eye.*)

WANDERER.
Smith of wisdom, hail !
The weary guest
welcome give
to house and hearth !

MIME
(*has started up in alarm*).
Who far in the forest
follows me so,
who besets me in wayless woods ?

WANDERER.
Wanderer calls me the world ;
far I've carried my feet,
on the back of the earth
I have boundlessly been.

MIME.
So move on thy way
and wait not with me ;
if "Wanderer" calls thee the world !

WANDERER.
Where I go I am welcome,
gifts were made me by many ;
let him be like them,
who looks for luck !

MIME.
Mischief long
has lived upon me ;
lend not thy hand to my hardship !

WANDERER
(*coming further in*).
Much I followed
and much I found ;

matters of weight
unwound to many;
sent from men
what made their sorrow,
need that had gnawed their souls.

MIME.
If all thou hast spied
and hast spelt that is,
here aids me not spyer or speller.
Leave me lonely
and let me be;
loiterers badly I bear.

WANDERER
(coming again a few steps nearer).
Numbers weaned
their widsom enough,
but what they needed
knew no whit;
when they asked me
what were wisest,
meed they met in my word.

MIME
(more and more anxious, as the Wanderer comes still nearer).
Numbers beg
for bootless knowledge;
I see enough for myself;
I shall want not for wit,
with my share I am well;
I show thy wisdom the way!

WANDERER
(sits down by the hearth).
I sit at thy hearth,
and set in thy hand,
on wisdom-wager, my head.
Thy hand has won
my head when its wit
has failed to unfold
what fits thy plight,
and loose with its lessons the pledge.

MIME
(frightened and perplexed, to himself).
How help I my house from his look?
My questions' craft I must lean on!
(Aloud.)
Thy head hold I
for my hearth;
now win it forth with thy wisdom!
For three answers
think I to ask.

WANDERER.
Bound am I to bring them.

MIME
(after some thought).
On the back of the earth
has thy beat been endless,
and broad thy way in the world;
now cunningly tell
to me what kin
dwells in its covering deepness?

WANDERER.
In its depth and dark
is Nibelungs' dwelling,
Nibelheim home they name.
Dark-elves we deem them;
Dark-Alberich
daunted them once to his will;
with the might of runes
that ran in his ring
forced he the restless folk.
Glancing gold
in greatening hoard
for him they heaped;
the world it was needed to win him.—
What question is next to come?

MIME
(falling into deeper thought).
News out of
the navel-nest
of the earth I own thou know'st ;—
but break to me now
the breed whose bulk
burdens her shaggy shoulders.

WANDERER.
On her harbouring back
the heels of the giants are heard ;
Riesenheim's realm is their home.
Fasolt and Fafner,
their grasping masters,
grudged at the Nibelung's might,
till their hands in the matchless
hoard they had mixed,
and reached among it the ring ;
between the brothers
it bred a broil
that Fasolt fell in ;
in guise of Worm
Fafner is guard to the gold.—
Now threats of thy questions the third.

MIME
(who has fallen quite into a dream).
True tidings
thou also tell'st
of the earth's unshapen shoulders ;
now last I will learn
the race that aloof
rules in heights that are hidden ?

WANDERER.
Of heights that are hid
gods are the holders;
Walhall's hall is their home.
Light-elves we own them ;
Light-Alberich,
Wotan, leads them his way.

From the world-ash's
holiest arm
he shore for his hold a shaft;
though starves the stem,
still unspoiled is the spear;
and with its point
pins Wotan the world.
Runes of blest
unrending bargains
hewn in it bears the handle;
the world in heed
waits at the hand,
where the spear fits
that fist of Wotan feels.
His nod withholds
the Nibelungs' host;
the giants he made
meek to his mind;
endlessly all to him hearken
whose span upholds the spear.

(*He strikes, as if involuntarily, on the ground with his spear; faint thunder is heard, at which Mime is violently frightened.*)

How deem'st thou, wily dwarf?
Quit I thy questions well?
Unwon have I held my head?

MIME

(*has started out of his dreamy forgetfulness, and appears troubled, without daring to look at the Wanderer*).

Questions and head
loosest thou whole;
so, Wanderer, hence on thy way!

WANDERER.

What is well for thy ear
wert thou to ask me;
and held'st, till I answered, my head;
that thy nearest need
scarcely thou know'st,
now put I thy skull into pawn.

   Greeted not
   gladly as guest,
   my head I straight
   staked in thy hand,
to get the good of thy hearth.
   By wager's force
   forfeit thou fall'st,
   can'st thou not meet
   three questions of mine;
so waken, Mime, thy wit!

     MIME
  (*shyly, and with timid resignation*).
   Long from my land
   of home I have lived,
   miles I've wandered
   from my mother's womb;
the eyelight of Wotan opened,
my walls were live with his look;
   before him withers
   my mother-wit.
But well it becomes to be wise!
Wanderer, question away!
The dwarf, driven to risk it,
may ransom perhaps his head.

     WANDERER.
First, trustworthy dwarf,
   truthfully tell me,
what is the name of the race
where Wotan wreaks his wrath,
meanwhile though he loves it like life?

     MIME.
   Heroes' breeds
   I but barely hear of,
yet easily answer thee here.
   The Wolsungs were raised
   to work his wish,
   begot by Wotan
   and greatly loved,
though reached them at last his rage.

Wälse was sire
of Siegmund and Sieglind',
the wildly treated
and woeful twins;
Siegfried leapt from their love,
the strongest shoot of the stem.

Withhold I, Wand'rer,
for once my head?

WANDERER.

Rightly thou readest
the name of the race;
sly I see is the rascal!
The foremost question
is fairly quit;
and now thou art free for the next;—
a knowing Niblung
nurses Siegfried,
Fafner soon he shall fell him,
that the ring he may seize
and rest on the hoard his hand.
Say what sword
is Siegfried to draw,
fitting for Fafner's death?

MIME
(*more and more forgetful of his present situation, and deeply interested in the subject*).

Nothung is named
a sundering sword;
in an ash's stem
Wotan stuck it;
he only should own it,
whose hand could haul it out.
The strongest heroes
left it unstirred;
sinews of none
but Siegmund served;
well he flashed it in fight,
till it split upon Wotan's spear.

Siegfried.

Now a cunning craftsman
the splinters keeps;
for he sees that alone
with the Wotan-sword,
a bold and witless boy,
Siegfried, will slay the Worm.
　　(*With satisfaction.*)
To guard my head
again have I happed?

　　WANDERER.
The wit of the world
is mean to thy wisdom;
who comes there to match thy craft?
But hast thou the brains
to build by the hand
of a boyish hero thy business,—
for thy other answer
now I ask!—
Say to me, wary
weapon-smith,
by whom, from his weighty halves,
is Nothung anew to be welded?

　　MIME
　(*starts up in extreme terror*).
The splinters! The sword!
Why spin my senses?—
What dare I do?
What must I deem?
The cursed steel,
for me to have stolen!
It fixes me wholly
in harm and fear;
its hardness holds,
it will not be hammered;
solder and rivet
set me not right.
The wiliest smith
smites it in waste;

who'll forge it afresh,
when I have failed?
The wonder—how shall I hear it?

WANDERER
(has risen from his seat by the hearth).
Thrice thou camest with questions,
three I manfully met ;
    thou sentest unfitly
    far thy search ;
but what was nearest thy need—
what thy want is, saw not thy sense.
    When now I name it
    wander thy wits,
    and here I have won
    in its wisdom thy head.—
Hark, dauntless feller of Fafner,
heed, thou forfeited dwarf ;—
    none but his fist
    who never feared,
Nothung welds anew.
(Mime stares stupidly at him ; he turns to go.)
    Thy crafty head
    keep as thou can'st,
in forfeit fallen to him
who is hid from hint of fear.
(He laughs and goes into the wood.)

MIME
(has sunk, as if quite crushed, back on the stool behind the anvil, he stares vacantly out into the sunny wood. After a considerable silence he is seized with violent trembling).
    How wide a flame !
    The wind is on fire !
    What flickers and flutters,
    what crackles and flares,
    what hovers and rocks
    and hurls itself round ?
    It glances and shoots
    in the gleaming sun !

What whistles and hums
and whizzes here?
It wades through the wood
and makes this way!
It roars like mad
and rushes at me!
Unmeasuredly gapes
a merciless mouth!—
The Worm will be with me!
Fafner! Fafner!
(*He shrieks and falls down behind the broad anvil.*)

SIEGFRIED
(*bursts out of the thicket, and calls from without*).
What ho! Thou idler!
Hast thou not ended?
Say what hap with the sword?
(*He has come in and stands in wonder.*)
Why fails the smith?
Forth is he fled?
Hihi! Mime, thou muddler!
What mean'st thou? Where hides thy
head?

MIME
(*with faint voice behind the anvil*).
Child, is it thou?
No one but thee?

SIEGFRIED.

Under the anvil!
So—what is it thou seekest?
Set is the edge on the sword?

MIME
(*in greatest trouble and distraction*).
The sword? How might I
see to mend it?—
(*Half to himself.*)
" None but his fist
" who never feared,
" Nothung welds anew."—

Too wise I waxed
for such a work!

SIEGFRIED.

Wilt thou not tell me?
Word shall I teach thee?

MIME
(as before).
From whence can counsel be called?—
My wily head
went in a wager,
and forfeit has fallen to him,
" who is hid from hint of fear."—

SIEGFRIED
(impatiently).
Seek'st thou to shuffle?
Shirkest thou so?

MIME
(gradually somewhat collecting himself).
I'd fly him now
who knows of fear;
but I left it afar from thy lessons;
forgot like a fool
the fittest good;
love for me
I longed he should master;
but, alas, my luck was bad!
Will better befall me with fear?

SIEGFRIED
(seizes him).
Out must I draw thee?
What did'st thou to-day?

MIME.

I sank in myself,
by way of thy safety
something to work that is weighty.

SIEGFRIED
(*laughing*).
Till under the seat
sunken thou wert;
what fetched thee so far with its weight?

MIME
(*recovering himself more and more*).
I look for the fear that thou lackest;
fast it befits thee to learn it!

SIEGFRIED.
So needful why looks it?

MIME.
Thou knowest it not,
and wilt from the wood
forth to the world?
What good were the soundest of swords
grasped without fright or fear?

SIEGFRIED
(*impatiently*).
Rotten counsel
comes of thy care!

MIME.
With thy mother's mind
warns thee my mouth;
good I must make
words that I gave her—
from the craft of the world
to keep thee in cover,
till fear thou had'st caught of its face.

SIEGFRIED.
Nam'st thou an art,
why know I it not?—
Unfold it now to me fully!

MIME.
(with growing animation).

Hast thou not felt
in furthest wood,
at gloomy spots
as twilight spreads,
when far it hisses,
hums and howls,
now with cries
and crashes nears,
fiercely flares
at thee, and flickers,
storms and swells,
and sweeps and strikes,—
hast thou not felt the hand
of horror along thy limbs,—
shuddering fire
shake thee to shivers,
wildly swim
and wander thy senses,
in thy breast, hunted and hurt,
burst thy hammering heart?—
Feltest thou not the fit,
fear thou never hast known.

SIEGFRIED.

Sudden and nameless
such must seem!
Whole and fast
feels my heart to me here.
With its shocks and its shudders,
showers and shivers,
fires and hurries,
flurries and hammers—
fear were worthy of wishes,
fast I would learn its delight!—
But how must I,
Mime, be helped?
Hast thou the means to be master?

MIME.

Lonelily let me
lead thee with me;
wholly I have them in mind.
I know of a wicked Worm,
who swallows what he sees;
Fafner is meet for a master;
follow me now to his nest.

SIEGFRIED.

Where holds he his home?

MIME.

Neid-hole
it has for its name;
to east, at end of the wood.

SIEGFRIED.

Not far away from the world?

MIME.

To Neid-hole its fringe is quite near!

SIEGFRIED.

Then bring me briefly to-wards it!
   Fear shall be with me,
   then forth in the world!
So quick! give me the sword;
in the world soon I will swing it.

MIME.

The sword! O woe!

SIEGFRIED.

Where is the weapon?
Show it at once!

MIME.

The cheating steel!
I stand not a chance with the stuff!

No dwarf that hammers
can deal with its spiteful spell.
He, who knows not of fear,
were fitter help in the need.

SIEGFRIED.

Sleights has learned
the slippery sluggard;
how he has bungled
back he will hold,
in hope to mislead me with lies!—
Here with the splinters!
Hence with their spoiler!
My father's steel
fits to my strength;
myself forge I the sword!

(He prepares quickly for work.)

MIME.

Had'st thou but willingly
worked thy hands,
they here would have stood thee in stead;
but lazy ways
thou wentest at lessons,
and hence they little will help thee!

SIEGFRIED.

Where the master is bad,
were meeter the boy,
who matches the way of his work?—
Now make me room,
meddle no more;
or fall with me in the fire!

(He has piled a great heap of coals on the hearth, and keeps up the fire, while he fixes the pieces of the sword in the vice and files them to dust.)

MIME
(watching him).

What seek'st thou so?
Here rests the solder;
I brewed already the broth.

SIEGFRIED.

Bring not thy brew!
I'm sick of broth;
no sword with batter I bake!

MIME.

Thou wilt flatten the file
and ruin the rasper;
so madly why wreck the metal?

SIEGFRIED.

The sword asunder
to dust I will saw;
what is broken so I will bind.

MIME
(while Siegfried files on fast).
No wit is wanted,
I see, this way;
the fool is served
by his folly itself!
Mark how he toils
and moves his might;
he dwindles the steel,
and stays not for drought!—
Here am I as old
as oak or hole;
yet such I never beheld!—
With the sword his will
he safely will work,
fearlessly forge it sound,—
the Wanderer saw it well!—
How hide I now
my hapless head?
It forfeit falls to the lad,
learns he from Fafner no fear;—
but woe to-wards me!
Who'd settle the Worm,
were fear upon Siegfried to fall?
Who beside him reach me the ring?

The cursed strait,
where still I stick,
find I not blinding ways
the fearless boy to outwit!

SIEGFRIED
(has now filed up the pieces and put them into a melting-pot, which he sets on the fire; during what follows he keeps up the heat with the bellows).
Hi! say to me now
the name of the sword
that so into dust I have driven.

MIME
(starting out of his thoughts).
Nothung, such
is the name of the sword;
from thy mother I met with the news.

SIEGFRIED
(while he works).
Nothung! Nothung!
Sundering sword!
What shook thee so into shivers?
To chaff thy biting
blade I've chopped,
thy bran I cook in the kettle!
Hoho! Hoho!
Hahei! Hahei!
Bellows, beat!
Blow up a blaze!
Wild was once
in woods a tree,
in the forest the trunk I felled;
the brindled oak
to blackness I burned,
on the hearth I build it in heaps!

Hoho! Hoho!
Hahei! Hahei!
Bellows, beat!
Blow up a blaze!—

How fleetly kindles
the forest coal,
how fierce and glad it grows !
In sputtering sparks
it spits and spurts,
melts me the metal's spray.—
Hoho ! Hoho !
Hahei ! Hahei !
Bellows, beat !
Blow up a blaze !—
Nothung ! Nothung !
Sundering sword !
Now seethes thy splinters' spray !
Thou swimm'st in sweat
thou madest thyself—
I'll bring thee soon to a blade !

MIME
(*sitting apart, to himself during the pauses of Siegfried's song*).
He forges the sword,
and fells me Fafner ;
I see it all safely before ;
hoard and ring
he wrests from his hold ;—
how in hand shall I get the gain ?
I'll win them both
with wile and wisdom,
and hide from woe my head.
Worn when he seems with the Worm,
to his side I'll draw with a drink ;
from seasoning saps
I sorted together,
broth for his good I brew ;
but a sip or so
get him to swallow,
soundly to sleep he goes ;
with the sword he welds
for himself in his wisdom—
hastily root him away—
and welcome to ring and hoard !

Hi! wary Wanderer!
Found'st thou a fool?
Of his nimble wit
what weenest thou now?
Means and meed
myself have I made?

(*He leaps up with satisfaction, fetches vessels and pours spices out of them into a pot.*)

SIEGFRIED
(*has poured the melted steel into a mould and plunged it into the water; the loud kiss of its cooling is now heard*).

In the water flowed
a flash of fire;
harrowing wrath
hissed to his heat;
fixing winter he felt.
The stream, that he flung
in the startled flood,
flows not again,
straight grows he and stiff,
stubborn and gashing steel;
seething blood
shall bathe him soon!—

Once more for me sweetly
sweat, as I mend thee,
Nothung, sundering sword!

(*He thrusts the steel into the fire and makes it red hot. He turns then to Mime, who, from the other end of the hearth, sets a pot at the edge of the fire.*)

What puts the dunce
to do in the pot?
While steel I bake,
is broth thy business?

MIME.

A smith has met with shame,
the learner his master leads;
at an end is his art at last,
as cook keeps him the lad;

bakes himself iron the boy,
his elder brews him
broth out of eggs.
          (*He goes on with his cooking.*)

              SIEGFRIED
          (*still during his work*).
     Mime, the craftsman,
     minds the kitchen,
his forge befits him no more;
     I have sent the swords
     he made me asunder;
of his mess I mean not to sip.

     That fear I may learn
     far he will lead me,
in mind to find me a master;
     what he truliest knows
     he teaches me not;
in nought than a bungler he's better!

(*He has drawn out the red-hot steel and, during the following song,
hammers it, with the great smith's-hammer, on the anvil.*)
     Hoho! Hahei! Hoho!
     Set me, my hammer,
     a hardy sword!
     Hoho! Hahei!
     Hahei! Hoho!
Hahei! Hoho! Hahei!—

     Once blazed with blood
     thy fallow blue;
     its ruddy ripple
     reddened thy rims;
     cold found it thy laugh,
     who licked its fire low!
     Hahahei! Hahahei!
     Hahahei! Hei! Hei!
Hoho! Hoho! Hoho!
     The roasting blaze
     has burned thee red;

on thy wound the healing
  hammer works;
sparks thou spitefully pourest
at me who master thy pride!
  Heiaho! Heiaho!
  Heiaho! Ho! Ho!
Hoho! Hoho! Hahei!—

Hoho! Hahei! Hoho!
  Set me, my hammer,
  a hardy sword!
  Hoho! Hahei!
  Hahei! Hoho!
Hahei! Hoho! Hahei!—

  I spend my glee
  on the spouting sparks!
  The storm I kindle
  becomes the steel;
laughter runs in thy look,
though fiercely feigned is thy rage!
  Hahahei! Hahahei!
  Hahahei! Hei! Hei!
Hoho! Hoho! Hoho!
  Both heat and hammer
  helped me well;
  with blows of weight
  thy will I bent;
now shrink from thy flushing shame,
and be cold and firm as thou canst!
  Heiaho! Heiaho!
  Heiaho! Ho! Ho!
Hahei! Hoho! Hahei!

(*With the last words he plunges the steel into the water and laughs at the fierce hissing.*)

MIME

(*while Siegfried is fixing the welded sword-blade into the hilt; again in the foreground*).

He forges a shearing sword,
  Fafner to fell me,
  the Niblungs' foe;

I brewed a slippery broth,
   that Siegfried may follow
   when Fafner falls.
My guile must put me to good;
pay must grow to my pain!
   That my brother wrought,
   the glimmering ring,
   into which he spent
   a mastering spell,
   the glancing gold
   that has might to give,
   I've won it and wear it,
   I wield its weight!—
   Alberich's self,
   who irked me so,
   I drive to sweat
   and dig like a dwarf;
   as Nibelungs' lord
   light I below;
   with heed shall hear me
   all the host!—
   The unwaited-for dwarf
   in worship shall dwell!
   To the hoard shall god
   and hero haste;
   my nod shall work
   the knees of the world,
   my eye shall send it
   shivering on!—
   No more to toil
   has Mime the mind;
   he'll heap by others
   the holy hoard.
   Mime by mettle
   makes himself master;
   lord and owner
   and leader of all!
Hi, Mime! how met thee the luck?
Who looked it was left for thy meed?

SIEGFRIED

(*in the pauses of Mime's song, while he files and polishes and hammers the sword with the small hammer*).

  Nothung! Nothung!
  Brightening blade!
Behold thou art back in thy hilt.
  Wert thou in bits,
  thy wound I have bound,
no shock shall bring thee to shivers.
  For death of the sire
  was snapped the sword,
  with life from the son
  again it is sound;
it greets him with laughing light,
when it hews for him, home it shall go.—

  Nothung! Nothung!
  Welded and new,
to life again thou art given.
  Dead lay'st thou
  and done with long,
now lordly and fierce is thy flash.
  Break upon rogues
  with broadening blaze!
  Strike upon wretches,
  stagger their wrong!—
See, Mime, my smith;
so slices Siegfried's sword!

(*During the second verse he has swung the sword, and now strikes with it on the anvil; this is split into two pieces, from top to bottom, so that it falls asunder with a great crash. Mime, in convulsion, falls to the ground in a sitting posture. Siegfried holds the sword exultingly in the air.— The curtain falls quickly.*)

SECOND ACT.

Far in the forest. (Quite in the background the opening of a cave. The ground rises as far as the middle of the stage, where it forms a small platform; from thence it sinks again backwards towards the cave, so that only the upper part of its opening is visible to the spectator. To the left a wall of rock, full of clefts, is seen through the trees. Dark night—thickest over the background, where at first the look of the spectator is able to discern nothing.)

ALBERICH
(leaning against the wall of rock at the side, in gloomy thought).
In night and wood
at Neid-hole here I watch;
with ear in wait
wearily lurks my eye.—
Yearning day,
dawnest thou yet?
Wistfully winnows
the dark thy way?
(A storm-wind rises, on the right, out of the wood.)
What light yonder is loose,
higher glances
and hither gleams?
It flies like the flash of a horse;
wildly it breaks
way in the wood.—
Has found the Worm his killer?
Is Fafner's feller come?
(The storm-wind ceases; the light disappears.)
The light is lost—
the gleam goes from my look;
night is it anew.—
Who nears with shine in the shadow?

THE WANDERER
(enters from the wood and stops opposite Alberich).
To Neid-hole
I hied through the night;
who is deep in the darkness here?
(Moonlight breaks forth, as if out of a cloud suddenly torn, and lights up the Wanderer's figure.)

ALBERICH
(*recognises the Wanderer and starts back in alarm*).
Thyself showest thou so?—
(*He breaks out into anger.*)
What seek'st thou here?
Haste from my sight!
Be hence, thou shirker of shame!

WANDERER.

Dark-Alberich,
Fafner's door
finds thee a haunting friend!

ALBERICH.

Hop'st thou to fill
thy hatred with food?
Linger not here,
look for it longer!
Its spite thy falseness
fully has spent on the spot;
so no further
seek it henceforth!

WANDERER.

To heed I neared,
and not to handle,
who hems me on Wanderer's way?

ALBERICH
(*laughing maliciously*).
Thou mad meaner of mischief!
Were I yet for once
but as weak in warfare,
as when thy fetter found me,
how ripe to be filched
were again the ring for thy finger!
Beware! though thy skill
well I can scan,
where lurks thy weakness
long I lived not to wonder.

For gold I gathered
    thy debts were forgiven;
    my ring sweetened
    the giants' sweat,
who laid thy bulwarks aloft;
    what with thy builders
    was rightfully bargained,
by runes is sheltered well
on thy spear's unwithering shaft.
    Gettest thou once
    what as guerdon thou gavest,
by force again into freedom—
    the spell were spent
    in thy stubborn spear,
    and amid thy strain
    the might of the staff
that masters were spilt like spray.

Wanderer.

Not by runes of rightful bargains
    bound it from midst
    of mischief thy bent;
it stoops thee to me with its strength;
I ward it well for my strife.

Alberich.

    In daunting words
    thou wastefully dealest,
while dread is at home with thy heart!—
    By dint of my curse
    forfeit to death
is Fafner, the hoard's withholder;—
who shall afterwards own it?
    Will the gladdening hoard
be held again by the Niblung?
That sears thee with nameless sorrow!
    For once if I feel
    its weight in my fist,
judge if like witless giants
I wield my ransomed ring;

then—shiver the heroes'
holy upholder!
Walhall's heights
storm I with Hella's host,
the world steer to my will!

Wanderer.

So thy thought flatters;
I fear not the threat;
he wields the ring
who wins it away.

Alberich.

How darkly thou sayest
what I see like the sun!
Thy hopes on heroes'
babes thou hast hung,
who sweetly bloomed from thy blood;
fosterest boys like a father,
to pluck thee fruit in places
thou fear'st thyself to seek.

Wanderer.

With me—hold!—
haggle with Mime;
thy brother brings thee thy harm,
for he leads a hero along
to fell for him Fafner here.
Nought knows he of me;
for Niblungs' needs he is meant.
I give thee word of good;
follow freely thy gain!
Bend to me well,
be on the watch;
of the ring recks not the lad,
but Mime has learned where it lies.

Alberich.

From the hoard holdest thou thy hand?

WANDERER.

Whom I love,
he walks with his will to lead him;
to stand or to sink,
himself he steers;
little but heroes I look to.

ALBERICH.

I wrestle Mime
alone for the ring?

WANDERER.

Beside thee he only
seeks it at all.

ALBERICH.

And yet likely am I to lose?

WANDERER.

To loose the hoard
a hero nears;
two Nibelungs gape for the gold;
Fafner falls,
who the ring withholds;
let the hand have, that can reach it!—
Is more thy want?
The Worm awaits;
warn him from death away,
swiftly he deals thee the wealth.—
I'll wake him for thee myself!—
(He turns towards the background.)
Fafner! Fafner!
Awaken, Worm!

ALBERICH
(to himself in expectant wonder).
Can he mean so madly?
Make me its master?

(Out of the gloomy depths of the background is heard)

FAFNER'S
(voice).

Who slackens my sleep?

WANDERER.

To help thee in need,
  at hand is a neighbour;
thy loss of life he hinders,
buy'st thou of him the boon
with the hoard thy body harbours.

FAFNER.

What will he?

ALBERICH.

Waken, Fafner!
Waken, thou Worm!
A hero hither strides,
thy holy strength to withstand.

FAFNER.

He makes me food.

WANDERER.

Full is the youngster's might,
fiercely swings his sword.

ALBERICH.

The golden ring
  rouses his greed;
hand it for meed to me,
  I help thee from harm;
  thou savest the hoard,
and soundly livest long!

FAFNER
(yawning).

I lie and beset it;—
let me slumber!

WANDERER
(laughs aloud).

So, Alberich, missed thy aim!
Yet rate me rogue no more!
　A thing I warn thee;
　think of it well;
all is but after its kind;
and it—canst thou not alter.—
　I free thee the place,
　plant thyself fast!
Be bold with Mime, thy brother;
for so thou wilt serve thyself better.
　What's otherwise
　awake to as well!

(He disappears in the wood. A storm-wind rises and quickly ceases again.)

ALBERICH
(after looking long and fiercely after him).

　He rides with hasting
　horse on his road;
he heaps me with scath and scorn!
　But let them laugh,
　the loose-hearted
　and hard-hankering
　gang of the gods!
　I'll see them all
　safe to their end!
　As long as gleams
　the gold in the light,
last a watcher his wits!—
Let them wince at his war!

(Day begins to dawn. Alberich hides himself aside among the clefts.)

(Mime and Siegfried enter as the day is breaking. Siegfried carries the sword in a belt. Mime carefully examines the place, searches at last towards the background which—while the rising ground in the middle is later continually more and more lighted by the sun—remains concealed in dark shadow, and calls Siegfried's attention.)

MIME.

Behold the hollow;
rest is at hand!

Siegfried
(seats himself under a great lime-tree).
Here fits me to learn my lesson ?—
Far I have let thee lead me ;
all night in fullest forest
we fared with no one near ;
henceforward, Mime,
I meet thee no further !
Find I not now
what I need to know,
alone forth I shall follow,
and leave thee fully at last !

Mime
(seats himself opposite him, so that he still always keeps the cavern in sight).
Boy, believe me !
Learn'st thou not
thy lesson nimbly here,
in farther haunt—
at further day—
dear would its fruit be deemed.—
Mark how gapes
and grins the gloomy mouth !
Awake there sits
inside a wayward Worm ;
endlessly hateful
he is to behold ;
a threatening throat
asunder he thrusts ;
with hide and hair
the heartless dog
will bolt thee bodily down.

Siegfried.
His gullet's gape I shall fetter
before it so far will have gone.

Mime.
Scathing spittle
he scatters in spouts ;

soon as the slaver
soaks in thy flesh,
it sickens and sears it like fire.

SIEGFRIED.

To be spattered not by the spittle,
aside from his sight I shall spring.

MIME.

His wrinkled tail
towers in rings;
let it but reach thy limbs
and gird them round,
thy bones will be broken like glass.

SIEGFRIED.

As it swings, my eye will be on it,
so that it sweep me not up.—
But warn me at once;
has the Worm a heart?

MIME.

A wicked and hateful heart!

SIEGFRIED.

And bears it where
for each it beats,
other be he or beast?

MIME.

Why yes, youngster,
so wears it the Worm;
more known is fear to thee now?

SIEGFRIED.

Nothung's steel
if I stick in his heart,
will fear be the hint I follow?

So, old idler,
only such
is all that thy lead
can aid me to learn?
Halt with me here no further;
fear I am hopeless to find.

MIME.

Yet awhile wait!
What I have told thee
weigh for untimely talk;
his body here
thou'lt barely behold,
ere wit will be weak in thy head!
When astray is thy sight,
when staggers thy step,
when thy bosom hardly
bears thy heart;—
thou'lt heed how Mime has led thee,
and hate him no more for his love!

SIEGFRIED
(leaps angrily up).

No love will I suffer!
Said I not so?
Forth from before my look;
leave me alone;
for long will not stand it my strength,
turn'st thou to talk of thy love!
Thy wearisome nodding
and nasty winking,—
when will the sight
no more be seen?
When may I be free of the fool?

MIME.

Already I run;
I'll rest and watch the well.

Hold thyself here;
soon the sun will be high;
wait for the Worm,
from the hole he hither will wind,
through the wood
thrust his way,
to wet his thirsty whistle.

SIEGFRIED
(laughing).
Lay thy length at the well,
the Worm will be wanting not long;
Nothung's cold
I will keep from his kidneys,
till he is ware
of thy taste in water!—
So weigh soundly my words,—
sit not beside the well;
forth on thy feet
both fast and far,—
with me no more be found!

MIME.
But after the fray,
may I not fetch
drink to befriend thy dryness?—
Hail me aloud
long'st thou for help,—
or if fear should befall thee at last.
(Siegfried with an impetuous gesture motions him to go.)

MIME
(to himself, as he departs).
Fafner and Siegfried—
Siegfried and Fafner—
may each be eased of his foe!
(He goes back into the wood.)

SIEGFRIED
(alone. He seats himself again under the great lime-tree).
To find my father not him,
how happy at heart I feel!

At last the forest
is fresh and live;
at last laughs to me
light of the day,
for he's safe from my sight indeed,
not again to get to my side!

(A thoughtful silence.)

How seemed my father in face?—
Ha!—why, such as myself;
had Mime a son to be met,
must he not look
Mime's likeness?
None the less nasty,
grubby and gray,
bunched and bent,
limping and little,
as big in his ears
and as bleared in his eyes? . . .
Fie on the fright!
I'll meet his face no more.

*He leans back and looks up through the boughs of the tree. Long silence.—
Sound of the forest.)*

Less can I learn
what my mother was like!
Fails wholly
to find her my fancy!—
The gaze of a doe
doubtlessly dwelt
with full dawn in her face—
or something sweeter!—

But when in woe she bore me,
what brought her to death that day?
Is it that men have mothers
who all and always
die of their sons?
Such were sorrow indeed!—

Siegfried.

Ah!—might her son
his mother see!—
My—mother!—
My father's mate!—

(He sighs and leans further back. Long silence.—The singing of the birds at last fastens his attention. He listens to a beautiful bird above him.)

Thou winsome singer!
From whence is thy song?
Hast thou thy home in the wood?—
What stammers he still so sweetly?
To me something he says,—
perhaps—he has heard of my mother?—

A moody dwarf
muttered one day,
that the talk of birds
in truth can be taught,
their song made into meaning;
but what should seem the way?

(He muses. His eye falls on a clump of reeds not far from the lime-tree.)

Hi! I will see,
send his song
in the reed's sound to him rightly!
If straight, without words,
the strain I can waken,
sing his tongue to him truly,
I shall learn before long what he says.

(He has cut down a reed with his sword, and makes a pipe out of it.)

He stops and turns;—
my talk I will start!

(He tries with the reed to imitate the song of the bird; he cannot do it; he shakes his head often in discouragement; at last he gives up the attempt.)

It runs not so;
on the reed I wrong
the song of its buoyant sound.—
Bird, I will own
my ear is bad;
thy call ill it has caught!—

In shame I am lost
as he lurkingly listens,
I know he learns from me nothing !—
Better my horn
will be for his heed ;
from the stumbling stalk
I no more will stand.—
Now thou shalt see
and say if I know,
a sound that is fit for the forest.
I have lured for the face
of a friend with it long ;
no better I brought
than wolf and bear.
Hark, while I find
if here it will fetch me
a friend and lover at last ?

(*He has thrown away the pipe and blows now a lively tune on his little silver horn.*)

———

(*A stirring is heard in the background. Fafner, in the form of an enormous lizard-like snake, has raised himself from his bed in the cavern; he breaks through the thicket and rolls himself forward out of the hollow to the higher ground, so that he has already reached it with the foremost part of his body. He now utters a loud yawning sound.*)

SIEGFRIED
(*turns round, perceives Fafner, looks at him in wonder and laughs*).
The blessing I hoped
have I blown to me hither ?
The looks of a lover thou hast !

FAFNER
(*has halted at sight of Siegfried*).
Who is here ?

SIEGFRIED.
Ey ! bides there a turn
in the beast for talk,
from his mouth I may meet with tidings !—
Of fear nothing
at all I know ;
like am I now to learn it ?

FAFNER.

Thy mettle masters thee?

SIEGFRIED.

Mettle or mastery—
what matters?
But woe waits for thy body,
fail'st thou to bring me to fear!

FAFNER
(*laughs*).

Water I wanted;
and meat's by the way!
(*He opens his jaws and shows his teeth.*)

SIEGFRIED.

How sweetly thy swallow
takes to its song;
turns in its laughter
thy teeth to light!
Needs I must narrow thy gullet;
thy jaws are greatly ajar!

FAFNER.

For waste of words
it fits not well;
to gape and feed with,
the gullet's good.
(*He threatens with his tail.*)

SIEGFRIED.

Hoho! thou mad,
unmannerly host,
to fill thy maw
I feel no fancy;
fitting and fair I deem it
to fix to-day for thy death.

FAFNER
(*roars*).

Pruh! boy,
follow thy boast!

SIEGFRIED
(grasps his sword).
Bellower, catch him;
the boaster comes!

(He places himself opposite Fafner, who lifts himself further forward on to the high ground and spits at him with his nostrils. Siegfried springs aside. Fafner swings forward his tail to catch Siegfried, who avoids it by leaping over the back of the Worm; as the tail quickly follows and almost seizes him, Siegfried wounds it with his sword. Fafner quickly withdraws his tail, roars and lifts the fore-part of his body in order to throw himself towards the side with his full weight upon Siegfried; he thus exposes to him his breast; Siegfried quickly discovers the place of his heart and plunges his sword into it, up to the hilt. Fafner rears still higher with the pain and sinks, as Siegfried lets go the sword and springs aside, heavily down on the wound.)

SIEGFRIED.
Enough, blustering knave,
bears of Nothung thy bosom?

FAFNER.
(with weaker voice).
Thou hardy boy, who art thou—
to have hurt my heart?
Who darkened thy childish mood
to the murdering deed?
Unwarned bred not thy brain
what thou hast worked.

SIEGFRIED.
Much never I knew,
have heard hardly my name;
thy work was it that stirred
my mind to the merciless strife.

FAFNER.
Thou lad unlearned of thyself,
with sun in thy look;
whom thou hast murdered
hear from me.
The towering team that once
with weight had trodden the world,
Fasolt and Fafner,
the brothers both have now fallen.

For the gold that came
in curse from the gods,
Fasolt fiercely I killed;
the Worm who here
harboured the wealth,
Fafner, the race's last,
a rosy fighter has felled.—
Be on thy guard,
blossoming boy,
for harm awaits him
who holds the hoard;
who set thee blind to the deed,
he is busy himself for thy death.

(*Expiring.*)

Mark my meaning;—
hark to me!

SIEGFRIED.

The kin I am bred from
yet to me break;
wide, as thou diest,
deem I thy wisdom;
seek in my name the knowledge;
Siegfried—know for its sound.

FAFNER.

Siegfried . . . !

(*He groans, lifts himself and dies.*)

SIEGFRIED.

The dead can lift no darkness.—
My living sword
shall lead me alone!

(*Fafner, in dying, has rolled on to his side. Siegfried draws the sword out of his breast; in doing this his hand is wetted with the blood; he wrings his hand violently.*)

Like fire bites the blood!

(*Involuntarily he puts his fingers to his mouth to suck the blood from them. As he looks vacantly before him in thought, his attention is suddenly fettered by the song of the wood-birds. He holds his breath and listens.*)

  Something has turned
 the sound of the birds into tidings;
 words above me are whispered!
  Brought it about
   the taste of the blood?—
 How madly here he sings!
 Hark, what means the song?—

   VOICE OF A WOOD-BIRD
    (*in the lime-tree*).
 Hi! Siegfried shall have now
  the Nibelungs' hoard,
  for here in the hole
  it awaits his hand!
Let him not turn from the tarn-helm,
 it leads him to tasks of delight;
but finds he a ring for his finger,
the world he will rule with his will!

    SIEGFRIED.
  Thanks for thy bidding,
   thou thoughtful bird;
  fair find I its bent.

(*He goes to the cavern and passes down into it, where he at once completely disappears.*)

(*Mime creeps forward, looking cautiously about, to assure himself of Fafner's death. At the same time from the other side Alberich comes forward out of the clefts; he carefully watches Mime. As the latter, seeing nothing of Siegfried, turns himself heedfully towards the cave at the back, Alberich hastens towards him and stops the way.*)

    ALBERICH.
  How far slink'st thou
  slily so fast,
  slippery friend?

MIME.
My cursed brother
I craved to bring!
What bade thee come?

ALBERICH.
Greatens thy hand
to have my gold,
and gapes for my hoard?

MIME.
Speed from amidst it,
the spot is for me;
what makes thee its spy?

ALBERICH.
Mar I thy step
in matters of stealth,
that stir thy mind?

MIME.
What I have met
by wearing means,
must not be wasted.

ALBERICH.
Who was it that robbed
the Rhine of gold for the ring?
Who was it begot
and gave the spell to the gold?

MIME.
Whence had the tarn-helm
the hiding wonder it holds?
Thy wisdom was it
that filled with it thy want?

ALBERICH.
Whose hand would have forged it,
had I not furthered his hammer?
The ring I made
moulded thee first to the might!

MIME.

Where keep'st thou the ring?
To giants it came by thy kindness!
What thou forego'st
I have gathered here in my guile.

ALBERICH.

Of the youngster's hand
may I hope for no harvest?
It belongs to thee not,
the lad is himself its lord!

MIME.

I brought him up;
what he owes is it he brings;
of work and woe
the meed I have watched for, I meet!

ALBERICH.

For his nursing heed,
hankers the nasty
niggardly knave
at last for nought
to count lower than king?
The mangiest hound
might for the hoop
be meeter than he;
hope not to get
thy hand on its mastering gold!

MIME.

Then make it thine,
and guard with might
the matchless ring!
Master be;
but me meet like a brother!
Give me the helm
thou got'st from my hand;
hold to thy ring;
for, rightly halved,
best is the hoard for us both.

ALBERICH
(laughing scornfully).
Share with thee so?
Let the tarn-helm slip?
Thy sleight is sly!
Safe and kind
my sleep were seen in thy keeping!

MIME
(beside himself).
Make no bargain?
Share no booty?
Bare shall I be?
Gather no gain?
Lose and leave thee the guerdon?

ALBERICH.

Not a nail,
that's now in the hoard,
thou hast for thy hunger.

MIME
(in rage).
Neither ring nor helm then
reckon to handle!
Now, never I'll halve!
To my side for help
I Siegfried will hail,
with sweeping sword;
his ready hand
shall bring thee, brother, to rights!

ALBERICH.

Listen behind;—
from the hole ere long he is here.—

MIME.

Trash to have chosen
I trust in the child.—

ALBERICH

He took the tarn-helm.—

MIME.
And keeps the ring!—

ALBERICH.
Be cursed!—The ring!—

MIME
(*laughs maliciously*).
Get it, while here he can give it!
It may not be his to-morrow!
(*He slips back into the wood.*)

ALBERICH.
And yet to its lord
alone it at last shall be yielded!
(*He disappears among the clefts.*)

(*Siegfried, during the latter part of what has just passed, has walked slowly and musingly forward from the cavern with the tarn-helm and ring; he looks thoughtfully at his booty and stops again, near the tree, on the height. Great silence.*)

SIEGFRIED.
How they are good
I hardly guess;
I got them here
from the heap of golden wealth,
by kindly warning that came.
I'll wear them that well
of my deed they may witness;
their look shall unfold
how I lightened Fafner of life,
ere in fight he led me to fear!
(*He puts the tarn-helm in his belt and the ring on his finger. Silence. Increasing sound of the forest. Siegfried is again involuntarily attracted by the bird and listens to it with suppressed breath.*)

VOICE OF THE WOOD-BIRD
(*in the lime-tree*).
Hi! Siegfried is holder
of ring now and helm;
but trust in Mime
no more he may try!

Siegfried, sharpen thy sense
   to the truthless sound of his tongue ;
      what he means at heart
         thou can'st hear from his mouth ;
so helps thee the burn of the blood.

(Siegfried's expression and gesture signify that he has understood all. He sees Mime approach and remains in his position on the rising ground, without movement, leaning on his sword, observant and self-possessed until the end of the following scene.)

MIME
(slowly drawing near).
He wonders and weighs
   the booty's worth ;—
      waited there here
      a wily wanderer,
      loitered around
      and read to the lad
   the cunning of crafty runes ?
      Doubly deep
      must be now the dwarf ;
      his keenest loops
      he is called on to lay,
      that so, with sweetened
      and sounding words,
he may baffle the wilful boy !
   (He goes nearer to Siegfried.)
   Be welcome, Siegfried !
   Say, my hero,
help hast thou happed on tow'rds fear ?

SIEGFRIED.
My teacher truly has failed.

MIME.
But the winding Worm
   to death thou hast wounded,—
too free was he deemed for a friend ?

SIEGFRIED.

Though grim and dreadful he was,
his death wins me to grief,
while much harmfuller wretches
rest unmurdered behind him !
Who set me to slay the Worm,
my hate to him is the worse.

MIME.

But soft ! not long
I live in thy sight ;
with lasting sleep
soon will thy look be allayed !
For all that I wanted
thou wisely hast worked ;
and here have I but
to bring to my hand thy booty ;—
and in means I look not for failure ;
a fool thou lightly art made !

SIEGFRIED.

So plot'st thou to seize my plunder ?

MIME.

How said I so ?—
Siegfried, hear me, my son !—
Him and all his ways
always well I have hated ;
I bore not for love
with the burdensome boy ;
the gold here from Fafner's guard,
the hoard to free was my hope.
Let it at once
and willingly loose,
Siegfried, my son,
or mark for thyself—
thy life must not be longer !

SIEGFRIED.

To learn thy hatred,
lifts my heart;
but my life wilt thou have from me likewise?

MIME.

Who owns it my aim?
Thou hast heard me ill!
(*He gives himself most perceptible pains for disguise.*)
See, thou art weary
and sore with work;
seethes in thy body the blood;
freshening fulness
of frothy drink
lagged not my love to draw.
While thy blade was at bake,
I saw to the broth;
sip it and let
me seize on thy loving sword,
with hoard at last and helm.
(*He chuckles.*)

SIEGFRIED.

So both of my sword,
and the boon of its battle,
ring and booty, thou'lt rob me?

MIME.

Wrongly thou readest me still!
Totters and stutters my talk?
The greatest toil
I give my tongue,
the hopes that I hold
to keep from his hearing,
and yet the witless youngster
falsely fathoms my words!
Heedfully mark,
and behold my mind;
hearken what Mime means!—
Drink, and freshen thy dryness!

My draught has fed thee before;
  be it with moody,
  mannerless brow,
  all that I offer
at last is owned to thy liking.

        SIEGFRIED
    (without changing a feature).
Of a wholesome drink
  here I dreamed;
how hast thou brewed what thou bring'st?

        MIME.
  Hi! but try it;
  trust to my hand!
  In night and numbness
swiftly thy knowledge will sink;
  without watch or wisdom,
straight wilt thou be stiffened.
  Soon as thy heed
  halts—softly
I seize the hoard into safety;
  but if once thou awake,
  nothing can ward me
  out of thy aim—
wraps me even the ring!
  So, with the sword
  thou so well hast set,
  hence ere I go,
  I must get thy head,—
that rest with the ring I may have!
      (He chuckles again.)

        SIEGFRIED.
In midst of sleep thou wilt slay me?

        MIME.
What mean'st thou?   Sounded it so?
  I shall but hew
  from thy shoulders thy head!

For held I not near
so whole a hate,
nor had such a share
of hardship and shame
to veil with healing vengeance,
 it were light of my wisdom,
 if alive it left thee
to hamper my hand in the business
where Alberich also would be!—
 Come, my Wolsung!
 Wolf's-son, come!
Drink and do for thyself!
From further sip thou art free!

(*He has gone close up to Siegfried and reaches to him now, with repulsive importunity, a drink-horn into which he has previously poured the drink out of a vessel. Siegfried has already grasped his sword and now, as if in a fit of impetuous disgust, strikes Mime with a blow dead to the ground. Alberich is heard from the hollows, as he bursts into mocking laughter.*)

SIEGFRIED.

Taste of my sword,
sickening talker!
Meed for hate
Nothung makes;
work for which he was mended!

(*He seizes Mime's body, drags it to the cavern, and throws it in.*)

In the hole below
lie on the hoard!
With greed and guile
thou mad'st at the gold,
now sway without measure its sweetness!
To a wakeful warder
I help thy wealth;
wrap thee from robbers his heed!

(*He rolls the body of the Worm before the entrance of the cave so as completely to stop it up.*)

Begone as well,
gloomy Worm!

The flickering hoard
hold with the foe,
who had feet so fast on its road;
to rest I have brought you both!

(After his work he again comes forward. It is mid-day.)

Warm made me
the unwonted work!—
Fiercely blazes
my flowing blood;
my head blisters my hand.—
High seated in heaven
the open sun
sends its eye
like an arrow whole at my head.—
Shelter and coolness
will come if I keep to the shadow!

(He stretches himself again under the lime-tree. Great stillness. Sound of the forest. After a long silence.)

Again, my bird, to greet me
back from my long
burdensome leave,
send me loudly thy song!
On the branch thou sweetly
swingest above me;
with chatter and chirp,
thy brothers and sisters
abound on the boughs at thy side!—

But look,—I am alone,
own not others to love me;
my mother fled,
my father fell,
ere saw them their son!—
I dwelt with a sickening
dwarf at my side;
love was lost
between us little;
treacherous tricks
he tried on my safety—
and needfully now I have slain him!—

Bird, of thy friendship
I further will beg ;
wilt thou not bring me
the brother I want?
Hast thou the wisdom to help me?
I've lured him so long,
with unbrightening luck ;
hope I bear
thy hap may be better !
Already hast thou been right ;
so sing ! I hark for thy song.
(Silence ; then)
VOICE OF THE WOOD-BIRD.
Hi ! Siegfried the slippery
dwarf has slain !
Now, would he might win
the lordliest wife !
Afar she sleeps on a height,
a fire besets her hall ;
he baffles the blaze,
he wakens the bride,
Brünnhild' he wins to his breast !
SIEGFRIED
(with sudden vehemence leaps up from his seat).
O friendly song !
Freshening sound !
It sears its meaning's
might in my soul !
To heat it strongly
startles my heart !
What so can befall
with fire my senses ?
Sing it me, sweetest friend !
THE WOOD-BIRD.
To sorrow of love's
laughter I sing :
set with its gladness
grief in my song ;
who long, they can grasp it alone !

SIEGFRIED.

Wild welcome
rouses my wayfare,
right from the wood to the rock !—
But further tell to me
faithful tidings ;
her bed shall I find in the fire,
win and awaken the bride ?

THE WOOD-BIRD.

To win the bride,
Brünnhild' to wake,
no coward nears ;
none to whom fear is known !

SIEGFRIED
(laughs aloud for joy).

The foolish boy,
who is blinded to fear—
than I no other is found !
To-day with toil
I undauntedly tried
if Fafner was fitted to teach it.
I burn with delight
to have Brünnhilde's lesson ;
who leads me as far as her fire ?

(*The bird flutters up, floats over Siegfried, and flies away.*)

SIEGFRIED
(exultingly).

The road is ready before me ;
my feet shall run me
fast on thy flight !

(*He hastens after the bird.—The curtain falls.*)

THIRD ACT.

Wild country. (*At the foot of a rocky height which on the left ascends steeply towards the back. Night, stormy weather, lightning and thunder.*)
(*Before the entrance of a grave-like hollow in the rock stands the*)

WANDERER.

Waken! Waken!
Wala, awaken!
From lasting sleep
I lead the slumberer loose.
I lift thee with sound;
aloft! aloft!
From depth without name,
and darkness dimmer than night!
Erda! Endless
woman, awake!
From heart of thy hollow
swim to the height!
I sing to wake thee,
waste not my song!
From brooding sleep
I bring thee to sight.
All-weener
of ere-world wisdom!
Erda! Endless
woman, **awake!**
Waken, thou Wala! Awaken!

(*Light has begun to dawn in the cavern; Erda rises from the depth in a bluish gleam. She looks as if covered with frost; her hair and garments cast a glimmering light.*)

ERDA.

Sore strikes the song;
strongly works the wonder;
from watchful sleep
I waken away;
who sets my slumber wide?

Wanderer.

Thy summoner am I,
and strains I open
with strength to startle
what sloth of sleep has stayed.
The world with wayfare
deeply I've worn,
wooed it for tidings
and tried for words of its wisdom.
Filled with thy knowledge
none I have found;
thou hearest whole
what the deepness hides,
in haunt or hill,
wind and water, what heaves.
Where life is lit
thy breath is below it,
of breeding brains
thy thought is the bent;
nothing saves
its name from thy sight.
Tidings to take from thy knowledge,
I now unseal thee from sleep!

Erda.

My sleep is dream,
my dream is drift,
my drift is wielding of wisdom.
But while I wake not,
Norns are watchful;
they work at the rope,
and weave aright what I ween;—
the Norns are what thou needest!

Wanderer.

With noise of the world
the Norns are bewildered,
and nothing at end can they alter;
thy wisdom was it
that helped me with warning
how to hinder a wheel in its whirl?

ERDA.
Deeds of men
with darkness daunt my mind;
my wisdom itself
from might once suffered the worst.
A wish-maiden
I bore to Wotan;
he warned her hail
heroes for him to Walhall.
Bold was she
and wise to boot;
why chafe my ease
and choose to aid thee
not Erda's and Wotan's child?

WANDERER.
The Walkyrie mean'st thou,
Brünnhild', the maid?
She warred with the steerer of storms,
when his will he most strongly withstood;
what the wielder of war
had burned and worked for,
and yet forbidden—
with harm in his breast—
dared, in unfit
dream of his friendship,
to do, for boon to her fancy,
Brünnhild' in fiery fight.
War-father
fell on her fault;
her look he loaded with sleep;
on her height she slumbers hard;
she will not turn
until she awake
to the man who wins her for wife.
How should she mix in my help?

ERDA
(is sunk in thought, and begins after lengthened silence).
Wild seems it
since I awoke;

fast and fiercely
wheels the world!
The Walkyrie,
the Wala's child,
chafed in hampering sleep,
while slumbered her mother's heed?—
Who the scorn wakened,
he scaths it as well?
Who the deed unbridled,
he burns when it's done?
Who guards the right,
he galls it like wrong?
Whom oaths are safe in,
forswears he for sway?—
Send me hence from his sight;
sleep shall hinder my hearing!

WANDERER.

The mother speeds not from me,
while the might of the spell is mine.—
Ere-wisdom
wielded'st thou once
to sink a sorrow
in Wotan's venturing soul;
to fear of shame
and shelterless fall
awoke him thy word
until dread had darkened his will.
Art thou the world's
wariest woman,
give me the way
how to ease a god of his ill!

ERDA.

Not such
thou art as thou sayest!
What sends thee wildly to harass
the Wala here in her sleep?
Wilderer,
let me away!
Spare me the lasting spell!

Wanderer.

Not such
thou art as thou seemest!
Ere-mother-wisdom's
end awaits her;
thy knowledge at Wotan's
will is nothing.
Know'st thou what now he wills?
Let it seize
thy ear with its sound,
ere thou slide for ever to sleep!—

My grief that the gods
must wane is forgotten,
since my wish so wills!
What in strain of wildering struggle
I once unhopefully hailed,
fast and freely
here I help to fulfil;
swore I, in withering sickness,
to night and the Niblung the world,
the winsomest Wolsung
away I name it to now.
Whom I chose but never
have neared to be known,
a boy of nameless boldness,
at none of my bidding,
has reached the Nibelung's ring;
grudgeless as laughter,
glad like love,
he lames with his clearness
Alberich's curse;
for far keeps from him fear.
Her that thou borest me,
Brünnhilde,
he breaks sweetly from sleep;
wisely works
thy wakening daughter
a deed to unweight the world.—

So darken thy sight,
dive to thy slumber;
see in thy dreams my downfall!
To what, not to wane
from its youth, they waken—
yearns the god as he yields.—
So downwards, Erda!
Ere-mother-dread!
Ere-sorrow!
To sleep without end,
below! Below!—
My look on Siegfried lights.—

(*Erda sinks. The hollow has become again quite dark; the Wanderer leans himself against its rock and so awaits Siegfried. Faint moonlight partially lightens the scene. The storm ceases entirely.*)

SIEGFRIED
(*coming in from the right in the foreground*).

My bird unfolded his wings;—
with fluttering flight
and sounding song
he wafted me sweetly away;
but now I see him not near.
The rock I will seek
to reach by myself;
the road I learned as he led
I'll follow further along.

(*He goes farther towards the back.*)

WANDERER
(*remaining in his position at the hollow*).

How far, youngster,
flee'st thou beyond?

SIEGFRIED.

So some one speaks;
he'll speed me in my search.—
To a rock I fare,
whose rim is flooded with fire,
where sleeps a woman
I seek to wake.

WANDERER.
Who sent thee here
to harm her slumber;
who set thy will on the woman?

SIEGFRIED.
I heard from a hailing
bird on high;
he turned my head with tidings.

WANDERER.
A bird can chirp and chatter;
yet brings the sound no sense;
what moved thee to see
his song had a meaning?

SIEGFRIED.
The blood of a wild
unneighbourly Worm
I felled in fight before Neid-hole;
its taste had barely
burned my tongue,
when I saw through the song of the birds.

WANDERER.
But so to have slain him,
who made thee set
thy weight to the mighty Worm's?

SIEGFRIED.
I followed Mime,
a faithless dwarf;
to teach me fear was his fancy;
the blow however
that irked his breath,
down on himself he drew,
when he sundered at me his mouth.

WANDERER.
Who filled the sword
with sharpness fit
for a foe so strong to feel?

SIEGFRIED.

I forged it myself,
when the smith had failed;
or swordless I still had been found.

WANDERER.

But whence sprang
the mighty splinters
from which the weapon was made?

SIEGFRIED.

What matter to me?—
I know no more
than that fit they were for nothing,
failed I to weld them anew.

WANDERER
(*breaks out in joyous good-humoured laughter*).
So likewise I see!

SIEGFRIED.

What leads thee to laugh?—
Old asker,
come to an end;
keep me no longer to listen!
Be swift and show me
the way that I seek for;
but tells it nothing,
tie up thy tongue!

WANDERER.

Forbear, thou boy!
Old if I be,
with heed it binds thee to hear me.

SIEGFRIED.

Looks it not likely,
when all my life
my elder has always
barred my business?
Barely I've swept him aside.

Let me be hindered
here now no longer—
or thyself see to,
lest such, as Mime, thou meet!
(He goes up closer to the Wanderer.)
But what art thou like?
And wherefore live
in so wide a hat?
Why hangs it so far on thy face?

WANDERER.

I wear it in wanderers' manner,
when they meet the might of the wind.

SIEGFRIED.

But an eye below it thou lackest!
None else I know
can have knocked it out,
but one whose step
thou unwisely withstood'st!
Hold thyself off,
lest here in the end
thou lose the light of the other!

WANDERER.

I see, my son,
to help thyself,
where nought thou know'st, thou art handy.
With the eye's aid,
that is out of my head,
thyself thou beholdest its fellow,
that I saved to befriend me with sight.

SIEGFRIED
(laughs).

Thy wit awakens my laughter!—
But here no longer I hearken;
so show me sharply my way,
and be off at once on thy own!
For all else
I find thou art ill;
now speak or forth from the spot!

WANDERER.

Knew'st thou me better,
  hardy boy,
this hurt had'st thou forborne!
  Hard on my heart
are threats from one who so haunts it.
  Love is my wont
    to thy laughing ways,—
    still thou would'st ride not
    the storm of my wrath;
    thou overlordly
    lad I delight in,
bring me not to it now—
it would scath and scatter us both!

SIEGFRIED.

Dwellest thou yet
  dauntless and dumb?
  Yield, and beware me,
  for yonder the way
seems to the woman who sleeps;
  my bird had beheld it,
who briskly broke from me here.

(It becomes gradually again quite dark.)

WANDERER
(breaking out in anger).
He left thee to save himself;
  the ravens' lord
  he believed I was;
woe to him that they hunt!—
  The way that he showed thee
  thou shalt not walk!

SIEGFRIED.

Ho, ho! my forbidder!
  Who must thou be,
with right to bar my road?

WANDERER.

Cross not her ridge's keeper!
By me was wrapped
in her sleep the slumbering maid;
he that awakes
and openly wins her,
mightless makes me for ever!—

With floods of fire
the woman is fenced,
redly it rushes
and licks the rock;
he who finds the bride,
must face the heat of her blaze.

(*He points with his spear.*)

Heighten thy look!
Behold'st thou the light?—
How flies the flame!
How flares the flood!
Withering blasts
and wavering beacons
leap, with the cry
of their coming, below!
The full heat
will hiss in thy face;
the sucking fire
will sear thee to cinders;—
back, thou bridleless boy!

SIEGFRIED.

Aside, thou boaster, thyself!
Forth, where the flame is wildest,
to Brünnhild' I break my way!

(*He strides towards the rock.*)

WANDERER
(*stretching out his spear*).

Hast thou no fear of the fire,
my spear shall hinder thy speed!

Still masters my hand
the heft of might ;
the sword, that thou swing'st,
once shivered on this shaft,
and lo ! shall split
again on the lasting spear !

SIEGFRIED
(*drawing his sword*).
So my father's foe
here have I found ?
Lordlily lit on
my vengeance looks !
Hither thy spear ;
my sword shall hew it in halves !

(*He fights with the Wanderer and cuts his spear in pieces. A terrible thunder-clap.*)

WANDERER
(*giving way*).
Away ! my hand cannot hold thee !
(*He disappears.*)

SIEGFRIED.
With his sundered weapon,
slunk he to safety ?

(*With increasing brightness clouds of fire have sunk down from the height of the background ; the whole stage is filled as with a heaving sea of flame.*)

SIEGFRIED.
Ha, gladdening glow !
Lightening look !
Ways of fire
widen before me,—
In flame to be floated !
In blazes to fall on the bride !
Hoho !   Hoho !
Hahei !   Hahei !
Listen !   Listen !
A comrade I come to at last !

(*He puts his horn to his mouth and, blowing his tune, plunges into the fire. The flames pour themselves now also over the whole foreground.*

Siegfried's horn is heard, first nearer then farther. The clouds of fire move continually from back to front, so that Siegfried, whose horn is heard again nearer, seems to turn himself towards the back up the height.)

(*At length the fire begins to grow paler; it dissolves, as it were, into a fine transparent veil, which now also fully clears off, and discloses the brightest blue sky in broadest daylight.*

The scene, from which the clouds have entirely disappeared, represents the top of a rocky height (as in the third act of the "Walkyrie"); on the left the entrance to a natural rocky chamber; on the right broad fir-trees; the background quite open. In the foreground, under the shadow of a spreading fir-tree, lies Brünnhilde in deep sleep; she is in complete and shining armour of mail, with her helmet on her head and her long shield covering her.

Siegfried, in the background, has just reached the rocky border of the height. [*His horn had at last again sounded further off, till it entirely ceased.*] *He looks about him in wonder.*)

SIEGFRIED.

Wilderness happy
on high in the sun!—

(*Looking into the wood.*)

What waits asleep
in the shadowy wood?—
A horse, see,
hidden in slumber here!

(*He steps completely on to the height, and strides slowly further forward; when, still at some distance, he sees Brünnhilde he stops in wonder.*)

What blinds me with its brightness?
It strikes like the blaze of steel!
Stares me the fire
still in the face?—

(*He goes nearer.*)

Lightening weapons!—
Lift I their weight?

(*He lifts off the shield and sees Brünnhilde's face, which is still however, to a great extent, covered by the helmet.*)

Ha! A man in his mail!—
How sweetly moves me the sight!—
The binding helm
burdens his head!

Loosened it lets him
softlier lie.
(He carefully unfastens the helmet and lifts it from the sleeper's head; long flowing hair breaks forth. Siegfried starts.)
Ha! Behold!
(He remains lost in the sight.)
Billows of cloud
that brimmingly border
a lake of hazeless heaven!
Laughter a face
of fathomless sun
sends through the mustering mist!
(He listens to her breathing.)
With swell of its breath
the bosom is swung;—
break I the hampering harness?
(He tries with great care to unfix the armour, but in vain.)
Out, my sword,
sever the iron!
(He cuts through with tender caution the rings of the mail on both sides of the whole armour, and then lifts off the coat and greaves so that Brünnhilde lies before him in soft womanly garments. He starts up in surprise and wonder.)
No man it was!—
Maddening wonders
hap to my heart;
fiery sickness
falls on my sight;
my senses totter and turn!—
From whom shall I call
help to me hither?—
Mother! Mother!
Beware for me!—
(He drops his forehead on Brünnhilde's bosom. Long silence. He then sighs and starts up.)
How waken the maid,
to measure her look for its meaning?
To measure its meaning?
Blind to be made with the blaze?
Dare it be done?

The light were a death !—
What rocks and swings
and sways me around ?
Withering words
are said to my senses ;
my shelterless heart
shakes here in my hand !—
What makes me falter ?—
What means my faintness ?—
O mother ! Mother !
Thy manful son !
A woman sleeps by the way,
and flusters his soul with fear !—

How deal with my heart ?
How help the dread ?—
To awake myself,
the maid besides I must waken !—

Sweetly mocks me
her blossoming mouth ;
it moves for my kiss
to be made in its midst !—
Ah ! to be smothered
in warmth of its wildering smell !—

Awaken ! Holy
woman, awake !—
No look she lifts.—
For life I will suck
her lips of their sweetness—
or light in the deed upon death !

(*He kisses her long and fervently. He then starts up in alarm; Brünn-hilde has opened her eyes. He looks at her in wonder. Both remain for some time lost in the sight of each other.*)

BRÜNNHILDE
(*slowly and solemnly rising to a sitting posture*).
Sun, I hail thee !
Hail thee, light !
Hail thee, slumberless day !

Deep was my sleep;
its dreams are done;
warn me what hero
wakens me here?

SIEGFRIED
(*solemnly struck by her look and voice*).
I have fought the fire
of thy flaming height;
I unfastened thy holding helm;
Siegfried was it,
who woke thee so.

BRÜNNHILDE
(*sitting fully up*).
Gods, I hail you!
Hail thee, world!
Hail thee, earth in thy heaven!
At last my slumber swerves;
my sight leads me;
Siegfried is it,
who ends my sleep!

SIEGFRIED
(*in loftiest transport*).
The mother hail,
who made me a man;
earth, who fed
and fostered me on,
till here I lit on the look,
that laughs my heart from its harm!

BRÜNNHILDE
(*with greatest emotion*).
The mother hail,
who made thee a man;
earth, who fed
and fostered thee on;
for thy look only I lay,
to other would not awake!—

O Siegfried! Happy
hero to see!

Thou lifter of life!
Thou mastering light!
O wealth of the world, behold
how I have loved thee long!
Thou wert my sorrow,
and song as well!
I gave thee
unbegotten my guard;
unborn—in its shelter
bound thee my shield;
such was my love for thee, Siegfried!

SIEGFRIED
(softly and shyly).
So slept my mother merely?
Left a little her son?

BRÜNNHILDE
(smiling).
Thou capturing child!
Thou wilt come no more on thy mother.—
Thyself am I,
soon as thy love thou hast owned.
What thou not knowest
know I for thee;
and light is lent me,
because only I love thee.—

O Siegfried! Siegfried!
Wakening sun!
I loved thee always;
for I alone
of Wotan's aim was a witness;
that I dared not to know
by the name he dealt it;
that I might not fathom
and merely could feel;
for which I faced
warfare and work;
for which I thwarted
him who had thought it;

for which I suffered
shackles of sleep,
when I failed to think it
and only felt;
since to me wholly—
so must thou see it!—
like love for thee, Siegfried, it looked!

SIEGFRIED.

A wonder sounds
its word in thy song;
but dark I deem it of sense.
Below thy lids
I behold the light;
with the wind thy breath
has blown, I am warm,
that thy tongue is sweet
of sound I can tell;
but what thou say'st in thy song
hides from my wildered heed.
The farness but dimly
dawns in my fancy,
while all my senses
can see and seize on thee only.—
The clasping dread
clings like a dream;
no fear I felt
till I came to thy face.
Unfix my manhood
from might of thy fetters;
give it to freedom again!

BRÜNNHILDE
(*keeps him gently off, and turns her look towards the wood*).
—At hand is Grane,
my happy horse;
how sweetly he browses,
who by me slept,
for Siegfried awoke him as well.

Siegfried.
My look on thy lips
its hunger has lightened ;
with fathomless thirst
my mouth is on fire,
till the food of my eyes shall have fed it.

Brünnhilde
(pointing with her hand).
—And here is my shield,
that sheltered heroes ;
the helm that held
in its midst my head ;
it helps and hides me no more !

Siegfried.
I was harmed by a happy
maid to the heart ;
hurts from a woman
heaped on my head ;—
I shared not in helm or shield !

Brünnhilde
(with increased sadness).
Now meets me the streaming
steel of my mail ;
a shearing sword
sundered its seams ;
from the limbs of the maid
it is loosened and lost ;—
to the last I am stripped of my strength,
and am left a woman of woe !

Siegfried.
Through towering fire
I trod to thy face ;
my bosom of harbouring
harness was bare ;
deeply my breast
is drenched with the blazes,
to flowering flame
my blood they have flushed ;

it bites with withering
wounds in my body;
the heat, that branded
Brünnhilde's height,
has burnt me here to the bone!—
Thou woman, slacken its surge!
Weaken its maddening might!

(*He impetuously embraces her; she leaps up, holds him off with the strength of extremest dread, and flies to the other side.*)

BRÜNNHILDE.

No god's grasp have I met;
the heroes meetly
hailed me as maiden;
holy went I from Walhall!—
Woe! Woe!
Woe for the sheer
unwavering shame!
Who wakes the maid,
he wounds her as well!
He has broken harness and helm;
Brünnhild' no further is found!

SIEGFRIED.

Unmoved I deem
the maid from her dreams;
Brünnhilde's sleep
soundly abides.
A woman awaken to be!

BRÜNNHILDE.

My senses unsettle!
My knowledge sinks;
wanes from me now my wisdom?

SIEGFRIED.

What made thee sing
thy wisdom meant
the light of thy love to me?

BRÜNNHILDE.

Drearily loses
my look the day;
my sight is listless,
no light I see;
deep is the night;
a snake from the dark
dreadly is sent
to seethe and surge!
Horror hisses
and hurls up its head!
(*She vehemently covers her eyes with her hands.*)

SIEGFRIED
(*softly loosens her hands from her eyes*).
Night befalls
the eyes that are fastened;
with the fetters, dwindles
the fitful dread;
dawn from thy darkness and see—
broad is the blaze of the sun!

BRÜNNHILDE
(*in greatest distress*).
Sun, that swells
high for the sight of my harm!—

O Siegfried! Siegfried!
Hear me beseech!
Always was I,
always would be,
haunted with hope's
hungering sweetness—
and always to save thy ill!—

O Siegfried! Lightener!
World's delight!
Life of the earth,
and laughing lord!
Leave, ah, leave,
leave me unlost!

Force on me not
thy fiery nearness!
Shiver me not
with thy shattering will,
and lay me not waste in my love!—

Struck thee thy face
in the staying stream?
Stirred thee not sweetly the sight?
Once, if thou startle
the water to waves,
the floor of the flood
is broken and fled;
thy face falters and fades
in the blinding beat of its breast.
So leave it unwronged,
wreck not my rest;
let thyself—
seen in me so—
a glad and gladdening hero
hail thee on without end!—
O Siegfried! Siegfried!
Lightening lad!
Love—thyself,
and loose from my side;
O end not what is thy own!

SIEGFRIED.

I—love thee;
O love me no less!
No more am I mine;
be given to me!—
A freshening water
fills and flows;
with soul and senses
all that I see
is the bounding bountiful billow;
what if my likeness
is lost in the whirl?
Myself in the flood
I fling like a fire!

I spring from my spot!
I startle the stream!
O beat me with billows!
O swallow me sweetly!
My want shall sink in thy waves!—
Awaken, Brünnhilde!
Waken, thou maid!
Live to me! Laugh to me,
sweetest delight!
Be mine! be mine! be mine!

BRÜNNHILDE.

O Siegfried, when
was I not so?

SIEGFRIED.

Such as thou hast been
be to me here!

BRÜNNHILDE.

Thine only
I always will be!

SIEGFRIED.

All that thou wilt be
show me at once!
When I have felt
and folded thee fast;
beaten my heart
home at thy bosom;
blazed in thy glance
and gathered thy breath—
eye on eye—
mouth in mouth—
then mine thou art,
as always thou wilt be and wast!
But doubt is undaunted and deep,
till Brünnhilde burns like a bride!

(*He has embraced her.*)

BRÜNNHILDE.
Till Brünnhild' burns?—

Gone is my godly
rest and forgotten;
my faltering star
thunders with fire;
wisdom is caught
and whirled in a wind;
love with his laughter
strikes it like storm!—

Till Brünnhild' burns?

O Siegfried! Siegfried!
Where is thy sight?
With the blaze of my eyes
why art thou not blind?
Where my arm is set,
unseared is thy side?
Where my blood in its storm to thee
boundlessly streams,
the wasting fire
wilt thou not feel?
Failest thou fully,
Siegfried, to fear,
the mad mastering maid?

SIEGFRIED.
Ha!—
Now our hearts are hot on each other;
now our looks with answers are lighted;
now our arms are hurt as they hold us—
meets me again
my manful mood,
and the fear, alas!
I had failed to learn—
the fear thou had'st half
helped me to feel—
I find—like a fool—
I again have fully forgotten!

(*With the last words he involuntarily lets Brünnhilde go.*)

BRÜNNHILDE
(wildly laughing aloud in highest exultation of love).
O lordliest boy!
O lad without better!
Of highest deeds
thou heedless haunt!
Laughter leads me to love thee;
laughter lights me to blindness;
laughter we both will be lost in—
laughter shall fill our fall!—

Away, Walhall's
lightening world!
In dust with thy teeming
towers be down!
Farewell, greatness
and gift of gods!
End in bliss,
thou unwithering breed!
You Norns, unravel
the rope of runes!
Darken upwards,
dusk of the gods!
Night of annulment,
near in thy cloud!—
I stand in sight
of Siegfried's star;
for me he was
and for me he will be,
own and always,
one and all;
lighting love
and laughing death!

SIEGFRIED
(with Brünnhilde).
Laughter awakes
the woman to me;
Brünnhilde lives!
Brünnhilde laughs!—

Hail the sun,
that sees us here!
Hail the day
we behold in heaven!
Hail the blaze,
that of night is born!
Hail the world,
where Brünnhild' awakes!
She wakes! She lives!
She lures me with laughter!
Broadly strikes me
Brünnhilde's star!
For me she was
and for me she will be,
own and always,
one and all;
lighting love
and laughing death!

(*Brünnhilde throws herself into Siegfried's arms.—The curtain falls.*)

THIRD DAY.

DUSK OF THE GODS.

PERSONS.

Siegfried.
Gunther.
Hagen.
Alberich.
Brünnhilde.
Gutrune.
Waltraute.
The Norns.
The Rhine-Daughters.
Men. Women.

DUSK OF THE GODS.

PRELUDE.

On the Walkyrie-Rock. (The scene is the same as at the end of the second day. Night. Out of the depth of the background rises the glow of fire.)
The Three Norns. (Tall female figures, in long dark veil-like garments hanging in folds. The First, the eldest, lies in the foreground under the wide-spreading fir-tree on the right; the Second, younger, is stretched on a bank of stone in front of the cavern in the rock; the Third, the youngest, sits in the middle of the background on a rock at the edge of the height. For some time they guard a gloomy silence.)

THE FIRST NORN
(without moving).
What light lifts itself?

THE SECOND.
Dawns on us day so soon?

THE THIRD.
Loge's host
has heed, and reddens the rock.
Night is safe;
why spin we and sing we not now?

THE SECOND
(to the First).
What, while we sing to and spin it,
serves for rest to the rope?

THE FIRST NORN
(raises herself and, during her song, fastens one end of a golden rope to a branch of the fir-tree).
For grief or good to grow,
so set I the rope—and sing.—

At the world-ash
I wove it once,
when broadly stood
about the stem
its woods of whispering boughs;

in shade they shed it—
showered a well,
words of wisdom
went in its waves;
I sat and sang to its song.—

A dauntless god
drew for drink to its gleam,
where he left in endless
payment the light of an eye;
from the world-ash
ere Wotan went he broke a bough;
for a spear the staff
he split with strength from the stem.—

The wound, by dint of days,
deepened its way in the wood;
the leaves turned till they loosened,
drought dwindled the tree;
drearily waned
of its drink the well;
darkly swerved
and drooped my song.
For me to weave at
the world-ash is no more,
now fast to the fir
the rope for its rest I must fix;
sing, O sister,
—I send it so—
heard'st thou how it happed?

THE SECOND NORN
(*while she winds the rope thrown to her round a jutting rock at the entrance of the cavern*).
Binding runes
of unbending bargains
Wotan sunk
in the weapon's shaft;
he held with its hold the world.
A hardy hero
hewed the weapon in war;

in splinters bounded
the bargains' harbouring spear.—
Soon sent Wotan
    Walhall's warmen,
    the world-ash's
    withering arms,
with the stem, asunder to sever ;
    so fell the ash,
and wasted for ever the well !—
    I bind to-day
to the biting rock the rope ;
    sing, O sister,
    —I send it so—
deem'st thou why it's done ?

THE THIRD NORN
(catching the rope and throwing its end behind her).
    By giants built
    abides the abode ;
    with the gods and the holy
    host of his heroes
Wotan sits in the hall.
    In lofty layers
    lies the wood ;
    round the hall
    high they have heaped it ;
the world-ash once it was !
    Burns the heap
once holily, wildly and well,
    sears the heat
swiftly from sight the hall,
the end of the gods is on them,
upward darkens their doom.—

    If yet you know,
be ready anew for the rope !
    Again from north
    I give it thy grasp ;
spin, O sister, and sing !

(She has thrown the rope to the Second Norn, who has thrown it on again to the First.)

THE FIRST NORN
(loosens the rope from the bough, and, during the following song, fastens it again to another branch).

Day is it dawns,
or the flame is it flickers?
My look fails of its light;
no way behold I
such holy wont
as when Loge burned
lightly with laughing blaze;
heard'st thou what happed to him?

THE SECOND NORN
(again winding the rope thrown to her round the rock).

By his weapon's wonder
Wotan withheld him;
help he gave to the god;
on the runes that fixed him,
fiercely for freedom
fell the touch of his tooth;
till, with the wakeful
sway of his weapon,
Wotan for beacon
set him to Brünnhilde's slumber;—
heed'st thou what grows from him?

THE THIRD NORN
(who has again caught the rope, and throws it behind her).

With the shattered spear's
unshapen splinters
Wotan hurts him
once home to his fiery heart;
flows from the wound
withering flame,
that Wotan aims
at the world-ash
as it lies aloft in its layers.—
Seek you word
when such will be seen,
reach me, sisters, the rope!

(She throws the rope to the Second, who throws it again to the First.)

THE FIRST NORN
(once more making fast the rope).
The night wanes;
wisdom is with it;
I find no further
fitly the threads;
the rope is ravelled and thin.
A sickening sight
thrills and thickens my sense;—
the Rhinegold
writhes in Alberich's grasp!—
Tell what he turned it to!

THE SECOND NORN
(with anxious haste winding the rope round the rock).
The rock has tried
its tooth on the rope;
the strands no more
are steady and straight;
the web wildly is wound.
From wrath and wrong
rises the Nibelung's ring;
a wildering curse
works in the woof of the cord;
see'st thou what it will send?

THE THIRD NORN
(hastily seizing the rope as it comes towards her).
Too loose is the rope,
to reach the length!
Now ere I aim
the end of it northwards,
harder let it be hauled!
(She pulls strongly at the rope; it breaks in the middle.)

THE SECOND.
It parts!

THE THIRD.
It parts!

THE FIRST.
It parts!

(In terror, the Three Norns have started up, and come together towards the middle of the stage ; they seize the bits of the sundered rope, and with them bind their bodies to each other.)

THE THREE NORNS.
Away now is our knowledge !
The world meets
from wisdom no more ;
below to Mother, below !

(They disappear.)
(The daylight, which has at the last been gradually waxing, pours fully in, and dims the glow of the fire in the depth.)

(Siegfried and Brünnhilde enter from the cavern. Siegfried is in full armour ; Brünnhilde leads her horse by the bridle.)

BRÜNNHILDE.
From deeds and dangers,
dearest hero,
to hold thee long
how were it love ?
A single sadness
lets me linger ;
my worth so little
it was to win !—

From gods I had gathered
what I gave ;
rich was the hoard
of holy runes ;
but all the maiden
stay of my might
stol'n has the hero,
whom here I stoop to.—

Of wisdom bare—
though her wish abounds ;
alive with love—
though strength she has lost ;
let not the woman's
worth be little,
who grudges nothing—
but gives not again !

SIEGFRIED.

More gav'st thou, woman, to me
than well my grasp can wield;
and chide not, if thy lessons,
I own, are left unlearned!
The knowledge I need is mine—
for me Brünnhild' abides;
and the lesson was light that means—
mindful to be of Brünnhild'!

BRÜNNHILDE.

Seek'st thou thy love to send me,
be mindful but of Siegfried,
about thy deeds be mindful!
Forget not the girding fire,
that found thee swift and fearless,
when its blaze beset my bed—

SIEGFRIED.

Brünnhild' for bride to win!

BRÜNNHILDE.

Forget not the woman whose shield
was her wasting slumber's shelter,
till thou brok'st the hasp of her helm—

SIEGFRIED.

Brünnhild' for wife to waken!

BRÜNNHILDE.

Forget not the oaths
we gave together;
forget not the truth
we guard between us;
forget not the love
our life belongs to;
and Brünnhild' will burn unhindered,
hallowed and whole in thy breast!—

SIEGFRIED.

Love, ere I leave thee behind
in the holy fold of the fire,
for gift against thy runes
thou hast from my hand a ring;
of a deed I did the good
is guarded in its gold,
when I loosed from the world a Worm
who fiercely fostered it long.
Now mindfully treat its might,
as greeting got from my truth!

BRÜNNHILDE.

I grasp it as all my good;
for the hoop thy own is my horse!
Mixed he once his mane
in the wind at my warning—
    with mine
the might of his ways has waned;
    over streaming storms,
    through thickening thunder,
    no more
goes he as mate of the gale.
    But the way of thy feet
    —flows it with fire—
Grane ungrieved will follow;
    to thee, O hero,
    wholly he hearkens!
    Uphold him well;
    he heeds thy word;—
    O make to Grane
    oft greeting from me!

SIEGFRIED.

By might thou findest for me
must so my searches be furthered?
Is thy help to fix my fights,
will their fruit go home to thy hand?
With horse of thine to hold me—

in shelter of thy shield—
hereafter is Siegfried unseen;
I am but Brünnhilde's arm!

BRÜNNHILDE.
O were she the soul of Siegfried!

SIEGFRIED.
The heart I bear is of hers!

BRÜNNHILDE.
So wert thou Siegfried and Brünnhild'.

SIEGFRIED.
Where goes he both are together.

BRÜNNHILDE.
And my rock is bereft and cold?

SIEGFRIED.
It keeps both in its bounds.

BRÜNNHILDE.
O hallowing gods,
upholders of heaven!
Fix in your eyes
the unaltering pair!
Apart—set not asunder!
Asunder—put not apart!

SIEGFRIED.
Hail to Brünnhild',
broadening star!
Hail, lightening love!

BRÜNNHILDE.
Hail to Siegfried,
heightening sun!
Hail, lightening life!

BOTH.
Hail! Hail!

(*Siegfried leads the horse down the rock; Brünnhilde, in rapture, looks long after him from the edge of the height. From the depth is heard the joyous sound of Siegfried's horn.—The curtain falls.*)

FIRST ACT.

The Gibichungs' Hall on the Rhine. (It is quite open towards the background, which includes a free space of shore reaching to the river; rocky heights border the space.)
Gunther, Hagen, and Gutrune. (Gunther and Gutrune on the seat of honour, before which stands a table with drinking vessels; Hagen is sitting at it.)

GUNTHER.
Now, hark, Hagen!
Tell me with heed,
if Gunther rests at the Rhine
fairly to Gibich's fame?

HAGEN.
His name abides
thy grudgeworthy birthright;
who helped us brothers to birth,
Frau Grimhild' bade me behold it.

GUNTHER.
The grief is mine,
and groundless thy grudge.
Wield I birthright's boon,
wisdom lay in thy lot;
half-brothers' strife
never better was stifled;
and I call thy counsel fair,
when I ask it after my fame.

HAGEN.
Then foul it is found,
if ill is thy fame;
and worthy goods I wot of
by the Gibichung yet to be won.

GUNTHER.
To hide them brings
thy head to the blame!

HAGEN.
In guerdon of greenest summer
Gibich's stem I see;
but Gunther stands unwed,
and Gutrun's maidhood stays.

GUNTHER.
Whom fits it I should woo,
to further Gibich's fame?

HAGEN.
A wife waits thee,
like none in the world;—
on rocks her home is high;
in fire is hidden her hall;
who breaks through the fencing fire
to Brünnhild', he finds his bride.

GUNTHER.
And have I a heart for the deed?

HAGEN.
For a daringer doer it's held.

GUNTHER.
Who is the man with the might?

HAGEN.
Siegfried, the Wolsungs' son;
his is the help we want.
Of bridal twins,
the sister and brother,
Siegmund and Sieglinde,
best to his breed he was born;
in the wood he grew to his might;
for Gutrun's mate he was made.

GUTRUNE.
What deed did he so matchless,
that the mightiest hero he's deemed?

HAGEN.
At Neid-hole
was the Nibelungs' hoard
once held by a weighty Worm;

Siegfried muzzled
his measureless mouth,
and slew him with mastering sword.
Such was the sweeping feat
that helped to the hero's fame.

GUNTHER.

Of the Nibelungs' hoard I know;
is his the hold on it now?

HAGEN.

Who boundlessly wields its worth,
he bends at a breath the world.

GUNTHER.

And Siegfried found it in fight?

HAGEN.

Now are the Niblungs his slaves.

GUNTHER.

And Brünnhild' he only can win?

HAGEN.

At another wanes not her blaze.

GUNTHER
(rising angrily from his seat).

Thy gift is darkness and doubt!
The good I dare not gain—
to long for it hardly
lightens my heart!

HAGEN.

Let Siegfried bring her
to be thy bride—
were then Brünnhild' not thine?

GUNTHER
(disturbed, walking up and down in the hall).

What might is to send the man
to seek for me so the maid?

HAGEN.
Thy prayer would fail not to press him,
if fixed him Gutrune first.
GUTRUNE.
Thou mocker, harmful Hagen!
What means are mine to hold him?
Lordliest is he
of men alive,
the world's winsomest women
long will have lightened his want.
HAGEN.
In the shrine is a water shut;
who won it, believe me well!
The hero, for whom thou long'st,
leads it with love to thy hand.
Let him but light this way,
and drink of the draught that awaits him,
that he'd seen a woman before,
or sought the way to her side—
were soon forgotten and gone.
Now say
how Hagen's counsel sounds!
GUNTHER
(who has again approached the table and, leaning on it, attentively listened).
The meed is to Grimhild',
who made such brother mine!
GUTRUNE.
Siegfried well it were to see!
GUNTHER.
Where waits he to be sought?
HAGEN.
Rides he for deeds
unrestingly round,
a fencing wood
the world he will find;
the storm of his business will run him
to Gibich's strand on the Rhine.

GUNTHER.
Welcome is his at my hand.
(*Siegfried's horn is heard in the distance. They listen.*)
From Rhinewards winds the horn.

HAGEN
(*has gone to the bank, looks down the river, and calls back*).
Horse and hero brings a boat ;
his warning was it we heard.

With the labourless help
of a lazy hand,
straight at the stream
the boat he steers ;
such masterly aim
of the moving oar
warns of the fist
that befell the Worm ;
Siegfried is it,—safely no other !

GUNTHER.
Will he not wait ?

HAGEN
(*calling through his hollowed hands towards the river*).
Hoyho ! which way,
thou hearty hero ?

SIEGFRIED'S
(*voice, in the distance, from the river*).
To Gibich's hardy son.

HAGEN.
He sends thee greeting ; behold his hall ;
this way ; lay to and land !
Hail, Siegfried ! Welcome here !

(*Siegfried lays to. Gunther has joined Hagen at the bank. Gutrune perceives Siegfried from her seat, for some time in joyous surprise fastens her look on him, and, as the men then approach the hall, withdraws herself in manifest confusion, through a doorway on the left, into her chamber.*)

SIEGFRIED
(*who has led his horse to the land, and now lea is quietly on him*).
Which is Gibich's son ?

GUNTHER.
Gunther, I, whom thou seek'st.

SIEGFRIED.
Afar thy fame
has filled the Rhine;
now fight with me,
or be my friend!

GUNTHER.
Waive the war;
welcome hither!

SIEGFRIED.
Where house I my horse?

HAGEN.
His rest I heed.

SIEGFRIED.
Thou named'st me Siegfried;
met we ere now?

HAGEN.
Thy strength was enough,—
I knew thy stroke.

SIEGFRIED.
Guard well for me Grane;
thou hast not held
with bridle a horse
of happier breed.

(*Hagen leads away the horse to the right behind the hall, and speedily returns. Gunther walks forward with Siegfried into the hall.*)

GUNTHER.
My father's hall, O hero,
with gladness freely greet;
whither thou walkest,
what thou see'st,
of all I say thou art owner—

abode and birthright,
field and folk;
bind what I swear, my body!—
myself I make thy man.

SIEGFRIED.
Not field or folk I offer,
no father's house and hall;
left to me
were my limbs alone;
life has fed on them fast.
In a sword I wrought
are all my riches—
bind, my sword, what I swear!—
with myself I bring it the bond.

HAGEN
(standing behind them).
But the hoard of the Niblung
fame unfolds that thou hast?

SIEGFRIED.
Wellnigh I forgot the gold;
so—nurse I the needless gain!
To lie I left it in a hollow,
where a Worm its heap had watched.

HAGEN.
And nothing is with thee here?

SIEGFRIED
(pointing to the steel net-work that hangs in his belt).
Nought but this; I know not its worth.

HAGEN.
I tell the tarn-helm,
the Nibelungs' sheltering toy;
it helps thee when set on thy head,
in the shape thou would'st have, to
shown;

or, lures thee the farthest spot,
in a flash, lo it is found !—
And leftest thou all of the rest ?

SIEGFRIED.
But a ring.

HAGEN.
Thou wardest it well ?

SIEGFRIED.
It hangs on a woman's hand.

HAGEN
(*to himself*).
Brünnhilde ! . . .

GUNTHER.
No bargain seek to bid me ;
trash to thy treasure were set,
sold I for it all I own !
For his thanks Siegfried I'll serve.

(*Hagen has gone to Gutrune's door, and now opens it. Gutrune comes out ; she carries a filled drink-horn, and approaches Siegfried with it.*)

GUTRUNE.
Be welcome, guest,
in Gibich's house !
From his daughter's hand is the drink.

SIEGFRIED
(*bends friendlily to her and takes the horn; he holds it thoughtfully before him, and says softly*).

Were all forgotten
that thou gav'st,
one lesson haunts
my heart for life ;—
my earliest drink
to endless love,
with Brünnhild' alone shall be !

(*He drinks and hands the horn back to Gutrune, who, ashamed and confused, casts down her eyes from him.*)

SIEGFRIED
(with swiftly lighted passion fixing his eyes on her).
When so with thy light
my look thou hast seared,
why sink'st thou before me thy face?
(Gutrune, blushing, raises her eyes to him.)

SIEGFRIED.
Ha, sweetest woman!
Sweep me not so!
The heart in my breast
burns at thy beam;
my blood it has filled, whose billows
furrow my body with fire!—
(With trembling voice to Gunther.)
Say me the name of thy sister!

GUNTHER.
Gutrune.

SIEGFRIED.
Are good the runes
that in her eyes I unravel?
(He seizes Gutrune, with fiery impetuosity, by the hand.)
When thy brother's man I meant to be,
with pride he put me back;
would'st thou behave so haughtily,
said I to thee the same?
(Gutrune humbly lowers her head and, expressing by a gesture that she feels herself not worthy of him, with unsteady step again leaves the hall.)

SIEGFRIED
(attentively observed by Hagen and Gunther, looks, as if spell-bound, after her; then, without turning round, asks).
Hast thou, Gunther, a wife?

GUNTHER.
I never wooed,
nor lightly will
win me a woman's look!
On one my heart I have set,
that no wit can help to my side.

SIEGFRIED
(quickly turning to him).
With me for thy means,
what shalt thou miss?

GUNTHER.
On rocks her home is high;
in fire is hidden her hall—

SIEGFRIED
(with wonder, and as if to remind himself of something long forgotten, repeats softly).
"On rocks her home is high;
"in fire is hidden her hall" . . ?

GUNTHER.
Who breaks through the fencing fire—

SIEGFRIED
(hastily interrupting him, and quickly leaving off).
"Who breaks through the fencing fire" . . ?

GUNTHER.
To Brünnhild', he finds his bride.
(Siegfried expresses by a speechless gesture that, at the mention of Brünnhilde's name, all recollection entirely ceases.)

GUNTHER.
My feet will not lead to her lodging;
nor fades at my look her fire!

SIEGFRIED
(starting).
Me—frights not her fire;
I'll woo for thee the maid;
   for with might and mind
     am I thy man—
a wife in Gutrun' to win.

GUNTHER.
Gutrune then shall be thine.

SIEGFRIED.
Brünnhild' to thee will I bring.

GUNTHER.
But how wilt thou blind her?

SIEGFRIED.
By the tarn-helm's trick
thy likeness lightly I take.

GUNTHER.
The bargain swear to a bond!

SIEGFRIED.
Blood-brotherhood
breed with an oath!

(*Hagen fills a drink-horn with fresh wine; Siegfried and Gunther wound their arms with their swords, and hold them for a moment over the drink-horn.*)

SIEGFRIED AND GUNTHER.
Flowering life's
freshening food
far I drop in the drink;
brewed with heat
of brotherly hearts,
blazes the draught with our blood.
Faith I drink to my friend;
fast and fully
bloom from the bond
blood-brotherhood here!
Breaks a brother the bond,
fails in faith to his friend,
what in drops to-day
sweetly we drink,
in floods be sent from his side,
to right his friend of the wrong!
So—bid I the bond;
so—trust thee my truth!

(*They drink, one after the other, each half; Hagen then, who during the oath has stood leaning aside, with his sword, smashes the horn. Siegfried and Gunther take each other's hands.*)

SIEGFRIED
(*to Hagen*).
Why aidest thou not in the oath?

HAGEN.
My blood were ill for the cup!
  Not clean like yours
  and cloudless it comes;
  stubborn and still
  in me it stands;
my cheek it runs not to redden.
  So, far I bide
  from fiery bonds.

GUNTHER.
Leave the man to his mood!

SIEGFRIED.
  Fleetly afloat!
  My boat shall dance
with dipped brim to her dwelling;
  at the brink abide
  a night in the boat,
and the bride home thou shalt bring.

GUNTHER.
Wilt thou not rest awhile?

SIEGFRIED.
To be back again I burn.
(He goes to the bank.)

GUNTHER.
Thou, Hagen, shalt guard the hall!
(He follows Siegfried. Gutrune appears at the door of her chamber.)

GUTRUNE.
So fast, whither's their wayfare?

HAGEN.
Aboard, Brünnhild' to woo.

GUTRUNE.
  Siegfried?

HAGEN.
  See how he goes,
for wife Gutrun' to gather!
(He seats himself with spear and shield in front of the hall. Siegfried and Gunther put off.)

GUTRUNE.
Siegfried—mine!
(She goes back in great agitation to her chamber.)

HAGEN
(after lengthened silence).
So—heeded and safe
  hold I the hall,
harbour the field from its foe;—
  Gibich's son
  is gone with the wind;
a wife he's minded to woo.
  A sturdy hero
  bestirs his helm,
who deeds for him is to dare;
  he brings him his own
  bride to the Rhine;
but me brings he—the ring.—
  You buoyant brothers,
  boundless in sonship,
sing to your boat as it sails!
  Slight though you name him,
  you serve his need—
the Nibelung's son.

(A curtain is drawn together across the front of the scene and hides the stage. After the scene is changed, the curtain, which before closed in the foreground of the hall, is entirely withdrawn.)

(The rocky height, as in the prelude.)

BRÜNNHILDE
(sits at the entrance of the cavern and contemplates in silent thought Siegfried's ring; overcome with joyous remembrance she is covering it with kisses—when she suddenly hears a distant noise; she listens, and looks towards the side into the background).
Long unwonted delight
  whispers its way to-wards me;
  a horse I hear
  with heels on the wind;
  in the cloud he comes
  with storm to the cliff!—
Who stirs my loneness at last?

WALTRAUTE'S
(voice from the distance).

Brünnhilde! Sister!
Sleep'st thou or wak'st thou!

BRÜNNHILDE
(starts up from her seat).

Waltraute's cry!
With welcome it comes!—
Rid'st thou, sister,
rashly so to my rock?
(Calling into the scene.)
In the wood—
where was thy wont—
light from thy horse
and lead the runner to rest!—

Hie'st thou to me?
Hast thou the heart?
Giv'st thou to Brünnhild'
greeting dreadless of grief?

(Waltraute has hastily entered from the wood; Brünnhilde has hurried impetuously towards her; in her joy she does not notice the anxious shyness of Waltraute.)

WALTRAUTE.
Only to her
is it I hasten.

BRÜNNHILDE
(in extreme joyous agitation).

So seems it for Brünnhilde's sake
Walfather's bidding thou breakest!
Or what else? O say!
Were Wotan's will
softened to-wards my side?—
When against his godhood
Siegmund I guarded,
well had my fault—
I felt—but fought for his will;

that his fierceness was ended
fully he owned,
when he folded me so in sleep,
fettered me here on the height,
fixed me for maid to the man
who should find me and wake by the way,—
    to my bitter prayer
    yet bated his bent,
    with ravening fire
    feathered it round,
that cowards might keep from my rock.
    Safe for happiness
    held me my sorrow;
    the wonder of heroes
    won me for wife,
    and in his love
my lot is a laugh and a light.—
Lured thee, sister, my luck?
    To feed and freshen
    on what has befallen me—
halve my heaven—hast thou flown?

    WALTRAUTE.
    Mix in the madness,
whose fit makes thee a fool?
Not such was the hope that could drive me
in dread from Wotan's behest.

    BRÜNNHILDE.
    Daunts thee the fear
    that dreadly he follows?
Is his heart so hard on me still?
Thou heelest from stroke of his storm?

    WALTRAUTE.
    Fear of our father
were a cure fit for my care!

    BRÜNNHILDE.
Wonder I get from thy words!

WALTRAUTE.

Gather thy senses ;
hark, and heed what I say !
    Again to Walhall
    warns me the woe,
that from Walhall hunted me here.

BRÜNNHILDE
(terrified).

Is harm with the gods in their heaven ?

WALTRAUTE.

Take to thy soul what I tell thee !—
Since from thy face he was severed,
    to fight no more
    furthered us Wotan ;
    lost and lotless
wistfully led we to war.
Walhall's mustering heroes
    missed Walfather ;
    hard on his horse,
    without rest or roof,
unfollowed he went in the world.
Home lately he fared ;
    in his fist fast
were set his spear-shaft's splinters ;
a hero had hewn it asunder.
    With wordless hand
    Walhall's host
    he wafted to-wards
the world-ash with their axes ;
    he warned them to stack
    the wood of the stem
    till its towering heap
girded the hall of the gods.
    The gods at call
    came to his counsel ;
    his holy seat
    held him on high ;
    room beside him
rested for them in the sorrow ;

   in ring and row
the hall was filled with the heroes.
   So—sits he,
   and breathes not a sound,
   on stately stool
   uncheered and still,
   the splintered weapon
   fixed in his span;
   Holda's fruit
   no further he heeds;
   dread on the gods
like death begets its darkness.—
   On their feathers roused
   he forth his ravens;
   homewards again
with happy news when they hie,
   at length unsmothered
   his latest smile
grows on the lips of the god.—
   At his knees bewildered
   Walkyries waited;
   faint feels he
   the prayer in our faces,
   and all of us ails
might of a measureless ill.
   The tears I shed
   showered his shoulder;
   he faltered in face,—
and his thought on Brünnhilde fell.
Soon he endlessly sighed,
   sealed his eyelids,
   and, while he dreamed,
   he whispered in words—
" The day the River's daughters
find from her finger the ring,
   will the curse's weight
be cast from god and world ! "—
   His thought I read,
   and through the ranges
   of wordless warmen
   slipped from his side;

with stealth to my horse
I hastily strode,
and rode in storm to thy rock.
Now, O sister,
forsake me not;
meet are thy means,
withhold not the mood!
Finish the grief of the gods!

BRÜNNHILDE.
What tales of dreary meaning
tell'st thou to me like a dream?
With gods in heavenly
mist behind me
long my wisdom has lain;
I take no sense from thy tidings.
Wild and waste
seem they of sound,
while in thy look
the wan and wistful
fire wakens and fades;
with fitful cheek,
thou cheerless sister,
what seek'st thou wildly to say?

WALTRAUTE.
(in uneasy haste).
Here—on thy hand—the ring—
be ruled! hark to my hope!
For Wotan hurl it away!

BRÜNNHILDE.
The ring—from me?

WALTRAUTE.
The Rhine-daughters' make it once more!

BRÜNNHILDE.
The Rhine-daughters'—I—the ring?
Siegfried's seal of love?—
Leave thee thy senses?

WALTRAUTE.
Listen ! See me beseech !
  The world's woe
it grasps in width of its gold ;—
    fling it from thee—
    far in the water !
Save its sorrow from Walhall !
Let it cast its curse in the waves !

BRÜNNHILDE.
Ha ! knew'st thou now of its worth !
    Its meaning missed thee,
    feelingless maid !—
More than Walhall's welfare,
more than the good of the gods,
    the ring I guard ;
a look of its laughing gold,
a flash of its girding fire,
    gives the greatness
    of all the gods
in endless luck of their lot !
    In leap of its blaze
burns to me Siegfried's love ;
    Siegfried's love—
that words are not ready to witness—
such saves me the ring.—

    Begone to the holy
    hall of the gods,
    and read them a whispered
    word of my ring ;—
from love I go not with life,
no gods shall set us asunder ;
sooner shall Walhall's walls
    be dust for the wind !

WALTRAUTE.
    Such is thy trueness?
    So, in trial,
I learn the love of a sister?

BRÜNNHILDE.

   Hence on thy horse
   reinlessly home!
The ring thou win'st not away!

WALTRAUTE.

   Sorrow! Sorrow!
   Woe, my sister!
  Gods of Walhall, woe!

(She dashes away, and is heard swiftly, as on horseback, storming forth from the wood.)

BRÜNNHILDE

(looks after a hurrying, strongly-lighted storm-cloud, which is soon completely lost in the distance).

   Away in the wind
   thy blazing blackness
   streams with its storm;
to me no more will it steer!—

(Evening has gathered; out of the depth the glow of the fire rises more strongly.)

   Evening hastes
   to hide the heaven;
   faster flushes
my harbouring fire on high.—
   Why rears so redly
the beaconing billow its wrath?
   My farthest haunt
is filled with the hurry of flame.—

(The cry of Siegfried's horn is heard nearing out of the depth. Brünnhilde listens, and then starts with joy.)

   Siegfried! . . .
   Siegfried again?
How my soul gathers the sound! . . .
Up—early to greet him!
Into my god's own arm!

(She dashes, in the highest transport, towards the background. Flames leap up over the edge of the rock; out of them springs Siegfried up on to a high jutting piece of rock, whereupon the flames sink back, and again only glow up from the depth of the background.)

(Siegfried, with the tarn-helm on his head hiding half of his face and leaving only his eyes free, appears in the guise of Gunther.)

BRÜNNHILDE
(retreating in terror).

Who now ?   Is treachery near ?

(She flies into the foreground, and thence, in speechless wonder, fastens her eyes on Siegfried.)

SIEGFRIED

(remaining in the background on the piece of rock and leaning on his shield watches her for a long time; then speaks to her with a disguised voice deeper than his own).

Brünnhild' !   A wooer came,
that thy fire could not foil.
My wife I have fairly won,
so mildly follow me !

BRÜNNHILDE
(violently trembling).

Who is the man
with heart undaunted
in the highest hero's deed ?

SIEGFRIED
(still on the rock in the background).

The master Brünnhild' needs,
if binds her nought but might.

BRÜNNHILDE
(seized with dread).

A horror hovered
and struck my home ;—
the flight of an eagle
aimed at my flesh !—
Who is it harrows me ?

(Siegfried is silent.)

Man art thou merely ?
Near'st thou with Hella's
night on thy name ?

SIEGFRIED
(*after a further silence*).
A Gibichung am I,—
and Gunther is here the man,
who makes thee, woman, his.

BRÜNNHILDE
(*breaking out into despair*).
Wotan, thou fierce
unfatherly god!
Woe! Now I meet
what thy vengeance meant;
to shame and darkness
thou shoutest me down!

SIEGFRIED
(*leaps down from the rock and comes nearer*).
The night is near;
and rest in thy room
halves by his right thy husband.

BRÜNNHILDE
(*stretching up threateningly the finger on which she wears Siegfried's ring*).
Withhold! Turn from this token!
Thy hand shall show me no wrong,
while shelters me the ring.

SIEGFRIED.
Husband's-right it gives to Gunther;
with the ring wilt thou be wed!

BRÜNNHILDE.
Back, robber!
Bridleless thief!
And threaten me not to near!
Stronger than steel
makes me the ring;
who—rends it from me?

SIEGFRIED.

Unburden thee of it
bids me thy boast.

(He presses up to her; they struggle. Brünnhilde tears herself loose and flies. Siegfried pursues her. They struggle again; he seizes her, and drags the ring from her finger. She screams aloud, and, as if shattered, sinks down on the bank of stone in front of the cavern.)

SIEGFRIED.

I've made thee mine!
Brünnhilde, Gunther's bride—
bring me the way of thy bed!

BRÜNNHILDE
(half fainting).

O wisdomless woman,
what could'st thou ward?

(Siegfried, with a commanding movement, drives her forward; trembling and with unsteady steps, she goes into the cavern.)

SIEGFRIED
(drawing his sword,—in his own voice).

Now, Nothung, witness well
that faithfully I wooed;
lest I wane in truth to my brother,
bar me away from his bride!

(He follows Brünnhilde.)

(The curtain falls.)

SECOND ACT.

A space at the river-side. (In front of the Gibichungs' Hall; on the right the open entrance to the hall; on the left the river-bank; from this rises, diagonally across the stage towards the right in the direction of the background, a rocky slope divided by numerous mountain-paths; there is seen an altar-stone to Fricka with which correspond, higher up, a larger one to Wotan, and, towards the side, a similar one to Donner. It is night.)

(Hagen, with his arm round his spear and his shield at his side, sits asleep against the hall. The moon suddenly throws a sharp light upon him and his immediate neighbourhood; Alberich is seen in front of Hagen, upon whose knees he leans his arms.)

ALBERICH.

Sleep'st thou, Hagen, my son?—
Thou sleep'st, and hear'st me not,
whom dreams and sleep undid?

HAGEN

(softly and without moving, so that he appears still to sleep, although his eyes are fixed wide open).

I hark to thee, harmful Niblung;
what seek'st thou now to tell my slumber?

ALBERICH.

Forget not the might
thou hast means to gather,
bear'st thou the mettle
thou had'st from thy mother by birth.

HAGEN.

Though came my mettle from her,
my thanks hardly she kindled,
when caught her Alberich's craft;
wan and early old,
I hate what's happy,
mix not in mirth!

ALBERICH.

Hagen, my son,
hate what is happy!

Whom luck slighted
and sorrow settled on,
fitly thou lov'st me so!
Keep thy keenness,
feed thy craft;
the foes we war at
with weapons of night—
our hatred is hard upon now.
Who reft me once from my ring,
Wotan, the unwavering robber,
has met in his own
offspring his master;
by the means of the Wolsung
he wanes from his might,
and with all the gods together
in awe he waits for his end.
Him no more I fear;
fall he must with his fellows!—

Sleep'st thou, Hagen, my son?

Hagen.

Whose lot is to light on
what he has lost?

Alberich.

Mine—and thine
the world shall be made,
find I no fault
amidst thy faith,
feel'st thou my wrath and wrong.—
Wotan's spear
the Wolsung has withered,
who won the fight
with Fafner, the Worm,
and chanced like a child on the ring;
might he has reached
not to be measured;
Walhall and Nibelheim
wait for his nod;

at his fearlessness cowers
and falters my curse;
for the ring's worth
not a whit he reads,
in work wields not
its mastering weight;
buoyant delight of his life
burns him away like a brand.
    Him to undo
    is the deed that will help us . . .

hear'st thou, Hagen, my son?

HAGEN.

    His ruin to seek
    already he runs.

ALBERICH.

    The golden hoop,
the ring, have we to gather!
    A watchful woman
lives to ward him with love;
    drew, at her word,
    the River's daughters—
    who in drenching deeps
    once did me the wrong!—
again the ring from his hold,
my gold were hopelessly gone,
and no guile could bring it me back.
    So without rest
    seek for the ring!
    A son I begot
    and gave myself,
    from grief at heroes'
    hands to be guarded.
    Though wide of the strength
    to strive with the Worm,—
who was left for the Wolsung alone—
    to flawless hatred
    Hagen I fostered;

who now is to right me,
the ring to bring me,
though Wolsung or Wotan forbid.
Swear it me, Hagen, my son!

HAGEN.
The ring I will have;
harm not thy rest!

ALBERICH.
Swear it me, Hagen, my son!

HAGEN.
To myself I swear;
swerve from thy sorrow!

(*A gradually darker and darker shadow again covers Hagen and Alberich; from the direction of the Rhine the day is dawning.*)

ALBERICH
(*as he gradually disappears from sight, his voice also becomes fainter and fainter*).
Be true, Hagen, my son!
Trusty hero, be true!
Be true!—True!

(*Alberich has completely disappeared. Hagen, who has not stirred from his position, looks without moving and with vacant eyes towards the Rhine.*)
(*The sun rises, and is reflected in the river.*)

(*Siegfried suddenly comes forward from behind a thicket close to the bank. He is in his own figure, but has the tarn-helm still on his head; he takes it off, and hangs it in his belt.*)

SIEGFRIED.
Hoyho! Hagen!
Weary man!
Wake,—I am with thee!

HAGEN
(*slowly raising himself*).
Hi! Siegfried!
Thou hasty hero!
Whence stormest thou here?

SIEGFRIED.
From Brünnhilde's stone;
there was it I drew the breath,
with which I bade thee wake;
so fast I found my way!
Slowlier follows a pair,
with press of friendly sail.

HAGEN.
So brings he Brünnhild'?

SIEGFRIED.
Wakes Gutrune?

HAGEN.
Hoyho! Gutrune!
Hither! Haste!
Siegfried is here;
why hold the house?

SIEGFRIED
(turning towards the hall).
To both I'll break
the way I Brünnhild' won.
(Gutrune comes towards them across the hall.)

SIEGFRIED.
Give me thy greeting,
Gibich's-child!
To cheer thee, news of good I know.

GUTRUNE.
Freia welcome thee,
to fame of every woman!

SIEGFRIED.
Sweet now show
thyself and dreadless;
for wife I have won thee to-day.

GUTRUNE.
So leads my brother with him Brünnhild'?

SIEGFRIED.
Light was the woman to woo.

GUTRUNE.
Found he no harm from her fire?

SIEGFRIED.
Him it would hardly have stung,
had I not gone in his stead,—
to earn in Gutrun' guerdon.

GUTRUNE.
And no wound hast thou won?

SIEGFRIED.
I laughed as it washed on my limbs.

GUTRUNE.
Held Brünnhild' thee for my brother?

SIEGFRIED.
He was I to a hair;
the tarn-helm helped the deed,
as Hagen happily deemed.

HAGEN.
I gave thee word of weight.

GUTRUNE.
Thou mastered'st the fiery woman?

SIEGFRIED.
She failed at Gunther's might.

GUTRUNE.
And she made herself thy mate?

SIEGFRIED.
To her husband hearkened Brünnhild'
like a bride from darkness to dawn.

GUTRUNE.
And her husband here I see?

SIEGFRIED.
Where Gutrun' abode was Siegfried.

GUTRUNE.
But with Brünnhild' safe beside him?

SIEGFRIED
(*pointing to his sword*).
Between east and west is north;
so near—was Brünnhild' afar.

GUTRUNE.
How befell it that Gunther she got?

SIEGFRIED.
Through the lessening flow of the fire,
in morning mist, she let me
lead to the vale below;
    when near the strand
    we stood, like lightning,
Gunther straight to her leapt;
and I by the tarn-helm's wonder
wished myself fast this way.
A whistling wind now runs
our lovers along the Rhine;
so set their welcome at work!

GUTRUNE.
Siegfried, mastering man!
I fear thee for thy might!

HAGEN
(*looking down the river from the height in the background*).
With a sail the river is brightened.

SIEGFRIED.
And thanks its boder begs!

GUTRUNE.
True shall her greeting taste,
that gladly as guest she may tarry!
    The men—let Hagen
    hail to be merry
with wedding in Gibich's walls!

Laughing women
I lead to the feast;
my joy they'll unflinchingly join.
(*To Siegfried, as she goes towards the hall*)
Restest thou, harmful hero?

SIEGFRIED.
Rest it were to help thy work.
(*He follows her. Both go into the hall.*)

HAGEN
(*standing on the height, blows with all his might a great ox-horn, towards the land side*).
Hoyho! Hoyho! Hoyho!
You men of Gibich,
gather to me!
Woe! Woe!
Weapons this way!
Weapons! Weapons!
Guarding weapons!
Whetted weapons,
strong for war!
Need! Need is now!
Need! Woe! Woe!
Hoyho! Hoyho! Hoyho!
(*He blows again. From different quarters of the country trumpets answer him. From the heights and out of the valleys armed men rush hastily in.*)

THE MEN
(*at first singly, then continually more together*).
Why howls the horn?
Why wakes it to war?
It brings us with blades,
it brings us with weapons;
with biting weapons,
with wounding blades!
Hoyho! Hoyho!
Hagen! Hagen!
Fast the need unfold!
Name the foe that nears!
Who stirs the strife?
Is Gunther in strait?

HAGEN
(down from the height).
Hither with haste
and endless help!
Greeting is there to give;
a wife Gunther has wooed.

THE MEN.
Wants he a friend?
Follow him foes?

HAGEN.
A harassing wife
helps he home.

THE MEN.
He comes with her kindred's
shout at his shoulders?

HAGEN.
Fairly fares he,
frets him none.

THE MEN.
He had strength for the need,
withstood the strife?

HAGEN.
The Worm-killer
warded him well;
Siegfried, the hero,
held him safe.

THE MEN.
What help will he want of our weapons?

HAGEN.
Sturdy steers
he'll see you slaughter;
let Wotan's stone
be strewn from their wounds.

THE MEN.
Then, Hagen, what work for our hands?

HAGEN.
Upon Froh's a bristling
boar shall be felled,
and a goat to death
gashed upon Donner's;
sheep shall bleed,
in showers for Fricka,
that friend she be to the bridal!

THE MEN
(with continually increasing cheerfulness).
Slackens the business,
when beasts have been slain?

HAGEN.
In women's clasp
will wait the cup,
with mead and wine
mirthfully mixed.

THE MEN.
When horn is in hand,
what has to be done?

HAGEN.
Drink till the sweetness
has drowned your sense;
all to the gods and their glory,
that good they may be to the bridal!

THE MEN
(breaking out into ringing laughter).
Long luck and health
meets now the Rhine,
 if the harmful Hagen
 is merry of mind!
 The Hawthorn pricks
 and sticks no more;
 he hails us here
 to weddings instead.

HAGEN
(who has all the time continued very serious).
Now leave your laughter,
men of mettle,
and greet Gunther's bride;
Brünnhilde yonder he brings.

(He has come down from the height and mixed among the men.)

Hold to your mistress,
help her in harm;
frets her a wrong,
right it like fire!

(Gunther and Brünnhilde have arrived in the boat. Some of the men leap into the river and drag the boat to the land. While Gunther accompanies Brünnhilde to the bank, the men, with shouts, strike on their weapons. Hagen stands aside in the background.)

THE MEN.
Hail! Hail!
Welcome! Welcome!
Hail to Gunther!
Hail to his bride!

GUNTHER
(helping Brünnhilde by the hand out of the boat).
Brünnhild', your matchless mistress,
home to the Rhine I bring;
a lordlier woman
never was won!
Let Gibich's stately stem,
girded with strength from the gods,
to highest fame
fling up its head!

THE MEN
(striking on their weapons).
Hail! Hail to Gunther!
Happiest Gibichung!

(Brünnhilde, pale, and with her eyes fixed on the ground, follows Gunther, who leads her towards the hall, out of which now come Siegfried and Gutrune, accompanied by women.)

X

GUNTHER
(*stopping with Brünnhilde in front of the hall*).
Be greeted, hero, here!
My sweet sister, be greeted!
How meet thou seem'st beside
the man who has won thee for wife.
Two couples here blaze
with blush of one blessing;
Brünnhilde—and Gunther,
Gutrune—and Siegfried!

(*Brünnhilde starts with fear, raises her eyes and sees Siegfried; she lets go of Gunther's hand, strides with impetuous movement a step towards Siegfried, falls back in horror and gazes with fixed eyes at him. All are at a loss.*)

MEN AND WOMEN.
What bodes it?

SIEGFRIED
(*goes calmly a few steps towards Brünnhilde*).
What lames Brünnhilde's look?

BRÜNNHILDE
(*scarcely able to control herself*).
Siegfried . . . here! . . . Gutrune?

SIEGFRIED.
Gunther's winsome sister,
she that I wed
as Gunther thee.

BRÜNNHILDE.
I . . . Gunther? . . . thou liest!—
Why leaves me the light? . . .
(*She seems about to fall; Siegfried, being nearest, supports her.*)

BRÜNNHILDE
(*faintly and softly in Siegfried's arms*).
Siegfried . . . knows me not? . . .

SIEGFRIED.
Gunther, thy wife at something sickens!
(*Gunther approaches.*)

Awaken, woman !
Here is thy husband.

While Siegfried points at Gunther with his finger, Brünnhilde recognizes upon it the ring.)

BRÜNNHILDE
(with fearful impetuosity, starting up in terror).
Ha !—the ring . . .
his hand—behold !
He . . . Siegfried ?

MEN AND WOMEN.
How—so ?

HAGEN
(from the background stepping in among the men).
Hearken well
to the woman's words !

BRÜNNHILDE
(recovering herself, while she forcibly suppresses the most terrible agitation).
On thy hand here
I beheld a ring ;—
by wrong thou hast it ;
who stole it from me,
here stands the man !

(Pointing at Gunther.)

How had'st thou the ring
he wrung from my hold ?

SIEGFRIED
(attentively regarding the ring on his hand).
The ring from him
I never had.

BRÜNNHILDE
(to Gunther).
Reft'st thou from me the ring
with which thou mad'st me wife,
be roused and plead thy right—
gather thy pledge again !

GUNTHER
(*in great confusion*).

The ring?—No such I gave him;—
why guess thou see'st the same?

BRÜNNHILDE.

Why fails thee here the ring
thy hand so fiercely wrested?
(*Gunther, completely at a loss, remains silent.*)

BRÜNNHILDE
(*breaking into passion*).

Ha!—He then it was,
who tore my ring away,—
Siegfried, the treacherous rogue!

SIEGFRIED
(*who during the contemplation of the ring has been carried far away by his thoughts*).

No woman's help
won me the hoop;
from woman's guard
I grasped it not away;
from mind I miss not
the battle's meed,
that once at Neid-hole I met,
when I weighed my might with the Worm's.

HAGEN
(*stepping between them*).

Brünnhild', fearless woman!
Find'st thou in faith thy ring?
To Gunther gav'st thou the same,
him it beseems,—
and Siegfried has got it by guile,
for whose work he must suffer well!

BRÜNNHILDE
(*crying aloud in terrible distress*).

By guile! By guile!
Guile of shoreless shame!
By wrong! By wrong—
beyond vengeance's reach!

GUTRUNE.

By guile?

MEN AND WOMEN.
Who gets the wrong?

BRÜNNHILDE.
Gods of my heaven!
Holy beholders!
Was it your counsel's
whispered word?
Named you this sorrow,
unsuffered till now?
Shaped you this shame,
no shelter can shade?—
Find me a vengeance
unvaunted before!
Rouse me to rage
never wreaked on a wrong!
Brünnhild' bid
till her heart she has broken,
and home she has harrowed
his for its harm!

GUNTHER.
Brünnhild', be bridled!
Hear me, bride!

BRÜNNHILDE.
Away, betrayed
and tricked betrayer!
Hark to me, all;
not—him,—
the hero here
was it I wed.

MEN AND WOMEN.
Siegfried? Gutrune's lord?

BRÜNNHILDE.
He forced delight
from me, and love.

SIEGFRIED.
Fencest thou so
thy fame from sickness?
The lips, that falsely foul it,
fits it I teach how they lie?
Hark, if my truth I harmed!
Blood-brotherhood's
oath I bandied with Gunther!
Nothung, my shameless sword,
sheltered the truth I swore;
his sharpness meetly sundered
this woeful woman and me.

BRÜNNHILDE.
Behold how thy lips
heartily lie,
and witlessly seek
for witness thy sword!
He showed me his sharpness,
but likewise his sheath,
in which so sweetly
swung on the wall
Nothung, the watchful friend,
when his master had wooed till he won.

THE MEN
(running together in hasty anger).
Faith has he forgotten?
Fouls he the name of Gunther?

GUNTHER.
My fame is shaken,
shame is my share,
turn'st thou not back
the tale in her teeth!

GUTRUNE.
False is Siegfried
found to his friend?
Betoken that blame
blindly she brings!

THE MEN.
Wrong thee her words,
wipe them away;
shame back her summons,
swear us the oath!

SIEGFRIED.
Shame I her summons,
swear I the oath,
which of you wagers
his spear in the work?

HAGEN.
With my weapon's spike
I wait for thy speech;
that whole the oath may be held.

(*The men form a ring round Siegfried; Hagen stretches out to him the point of his spear; Siegfried lays upon it two fingers of his right hand.*)

SIEGFRIED.
Wakeful spear!
Hallowing weapon!
Help my unwithering words!—
By thy spiring spike
my oath shall be sped;
spear, behold what I speak!—
Where a blade can bleed me,
bite for my blood;
where a death can stab me,
strike me dead;
wrought I what rights her blame,
failed I my brother in faith!

BRÜNNHILDE
(*strides with rage into the ring, tears Siegfried's hand from the spear and seizes the point with her own*).
Wakeful spear!
Hallowing weapon!
Help my unwithering words!—
By thy spiring spike
my oath shall be sped;
spear, behold what I speak!—

On thy weight a welfare,
so it shall wound him ;
on thy blade a blessing,
so it shall bleed him ;
for broken are all his oaths,—
his last he breathes on a lie !

THE MEN
(*in violent tumult*).
Help, Donner !
Down with thy thunder,
to deaden the shout of this shame !

SIEGFRIED.
Gunther, look to thy wife,
who foully lies to thy fame !—
Rest she wants and room,
the wayward mountain woman,
till the maddening storm is stilled,
that some hand of hell's
unholy spite
opened for sport on us all !—
Be scattered, men, and away !
Leave the women to scold !
To count as cowards is well,
kindles the warfare with words.
(*Going close to Gunther.*)
Own, it irks me the worst—
that ill the sleight I worked ;
the helm, it seems almost,
but half withheld my mien.
But women's grudge
soon is outgrown ;
the trick, that won thy wife,
in time she'll think of with thanks.
(*He turns again to the men.*)
Fit me your faces,
men, for the feast !—
Light the wedding,
women, with looks !—

Loud with your laugh
make the delight;
in hall and field
fairly I'll hold
the front of jest and of joy!
Let the lucky man,
whose faith on love is fastened,
follow the mirth of my mood!

(*With unrestrained joyousness he throws his arm round Gutrune, and draws her with him into the hall; the men and women follow him.*)

(*Brünnhilde, Gunther and Hagen remain behind. Gunther, covering his face, in deep shame and terrible dejection, has seated himself aside.*)

BRÜNNHILDE
(*standing in the foreground and looking vacantly before her*).
Was the hand of hell
hidden behind it?
What's the spell whose spite
spurred it this way?
Why leaves me my wisdom
lone and bewildered?
Why falter my runes
to fathom the riddle?
Ah, sorrow! Sorrow!
Woe! Ah, woe!
All my wisdom
to him I weaned;
his maid he holds
hard in his might;
he binds his fetters
fast on the booty,
that, wild with cry of her curse,
he greedily gives from his wealth!—

Who brings to me here a sword
to sever the hampering bonds?

HAGEN
(*going close up to her*).
Let Hagen know
the whole of thy hurt!
For the wrong thou hast got
guerdon he wreaks.

BRÜNNHILDE.
On whom?

HAGEN.
On Siegfried, whose is the sin.

BRÜNNHILDE.
On Siegfried? . . . Thou?
(*She laughs bitterly.*)
At sight alone
of his gathering eyelight
—that even the garb of his guile
blinded ill of its blaze—
would thy meetest mood
find itself mastered!

HAGEN.
His vow will speed
my spear in its vengeance!

BRÜNNHILDE.
Vow and vengeance
help it in vain!
A weightier way
must thy spear be wielded,
seeks it with Siegfried to war!

HAGEN.
I know the might
and means of the man,
and deem not in fight to undo him;
so whisper me fast
of wary ways,
how he may wince at my hand.

BRÜNNHILDE.
O heartless meed that I meet!
Nought that I knew
left I unnamed,
when I blessing breathed on his limbs.
Heedlessly spent I
on him my spells,
that harbour him now from thy spear.

HAGEN.

So wounds him nowhere a weapon?

BRÜNNHILDE.

In battle none;—but still—
bare to a stroke is his back.
    Never—I felt—
in flight he would find
a foe to be harmful behind him;
so spared I his back from the blessing.

HAGEN.

For the bite of my spear!
(He turns swiftly round to Gunther.)
Wake, Gunther,—
    worthy Gibichung!
Behold thy helpful wife;
why waste thy heart in woe?

GUNTHER
(breaking out passionately).
O shame!
O sorrow!
Woe to me,
the wretchedest of men!

HAGEN.

In shame thou sittest—
such I see!

BRÜNNHILDE.

Unmanful comrade!
Cowardly man!
Meetly behind
the hero thou hidd'st,
that harvest of fame
from his hand might befall thee!
Far, in truth,
the towering tree
had fall'n ere thou wert its fruit!

GUNTHER
(beside himself).
Beguiled to be—and beguiler!
Betrayed to be—and betrayer!
It burns in my bone,
it heaves in my heart!
Help, Hagen,
bring to my fame!
Bring to thy mother's,
for me even—she bore!

HAGEN.
Not head nor hand
can deal in thy help;
thy help is—Siegfried's death!

GUNTHER.
Siegfried's death!

HAGEN.
Alone slays it thy shame.

GUNTHER
(seized with horror, staring before him).
Blood-brotherhood
swore we not both?

HAGEN.
The broken bond
heal with his blood!

GUNTHER.
Broke he the bond?

HAGEN.
When he mocked thy trust.

GUNTHER.
Betrayed he me?

BRÜNNHILDE.
Thee betrayed he,
and my betrayal you met in!

Wrung I my right,
all the blood that runs
would drown not the blame of your deed?
But by death of one
shall others be debtless;
Siegfried's end
shall settle his own and all!

   HAGEN
  (*going near to Gunther*).
His fall shall breed thy blessing!
Without measure might thou wilt find,
when lies in thy hand the ring,
that for death alone he will loose.

   GUNTHER.
Brünnhilde's ring?

   HAGEN.
That the Nibelung wrought.

   GUNTHER
  (*sighing deeply*).
Such were the end of Siegfried!

   HAGEN.
His death shall save us all.

   GUNTHER.
But Gutrune, ah!
to whom I gave him;
harm we her husband in this,
to her sight how seem we then?

   BRÜNNHILDE
  (*breaking wildly out*).
What reads me my wisdom?
What whisper my runes?
Through shelterless sorrow
shines it like sun;—
Gutrun', behold, is the wonder,
that witched my husband away!
Harm harrow her!

HAGEN
(to Gunther).
Deem'st thou it greatly will grieve her,
the deed from her can be hid.
    For merry hunt
    he meets us to-morrow;
his haste shall leave us behind—
a boar can bring him his hurt.

GUNTHER AND BRÜNNHILDE.
Such be the deed!
Death to Siegfried!
Harm that he sent,
so—let him heal!
From sworn truth
he swerved to betrayal;
now shall his blood
blot out the blame!
Allrauner!
Wreaker for wrong!
Oath-viewer
and aid of vows!
Wotan! Wotan!
Waken this way!
Hail to thy holy
harrowing host,
hither to hearken
and hear us swear!

HAGEN.
Such be the deed!
Death to Siegfried!
Soon shall he set,
who seems like the sun!
Mine is the hoard,
in might I will have it;
so wrung from him
must be the ring!—

Niblung-father,
who fell'st from thy fame!

Night-leader!
Nibelungs'-lord!
Alberich! Alberich!
Open thine ear!
Hail yet again
to the Nibelungs' host,
rightly to hallow
thy ruling ring!

(*As Gunther and Brünnhilde turn impetuously towards the hall, they are met by the issuing bridal procession. Boys and girls, waving staves hung with flowers, leap joyously in front. Siegfried, on a shield, and Gutrune, on a seat, are carried by the men. At the same time men and women servants, on the various paths of the rocky background, drive slaughtering implements and beasts for sacrifice, an ox, a ram and a goat, towards the altar-stones, which the women dress with flowers. Siegfried and the men blow with their horns the wedding-call. The women invite Brünnhilde to accompany them at Gutrune's side. Brünnhilde stares vacantly up at Gutrune, who nods friendlily to her. As Brünnhilde is about to retreat impetuously, Hagen steps quickly in and presses her towards Gunther, who again seizes her hand and leads her to the women, whereupon he allows himself to be lifted by the men. While the procession, scarcely interrupted, again quickly sets itself in motion towards the height, the curtain falls.*)

THIRD ACT.

A wild valley of wood and rock (by the Rhine, which flows past a steep slope in the background).

THE THREE RHINE-DAUGHTERS

(*Woglinde, Wellgunde, and Flosshilde rise out of the water, and, during the following song, swim about in a circle*).

  The sun has lit
   the land with laughter;
night lies in the water;
   it seemed not so
  when, holy and safe,
our father's gold was its gladness!
   Rhinegold,
    guiding gold!
How far felt we thy stream,
star that decked our darkness!—

   O send us hither,
    sun, the hero
from whose hand our gold we may gather!
    Brings he it back,
    thy blazing eye
grudge we at last no longer.
    Rhinegold,
     laughing gold!
How glad should we deem thy glance,
dancing star of our darkness!

   (*Siegfried's horn is heard from the height.*)

WOGLINDE.

His horn I can hear!

WELLGUNDE.

The hero comes.

FLOSSHILDE.

Hasten to counsel!

(*They dive quickly below the water. Siegfried, fully armed, appears on the slope.*)

SIEGFRIED.

Some elf has led me ill;
at last the track I have lost.
Hi, rogue! What harbour took
so greedily hence the game?

THE THREE RHINE-DAUGHTERS
(*coming up again*).
Siegfried!

FLOSSHILDE.

What here has hurt thee so?

WELLGUNDE.

Who's the rogue that set thee wrong?

WOGLINDE.

Was there a Nodder at work?

ALL THREE.

Say it, Siegfried; let us know!

SIEGFRIED
(*smiling and watching them*).
Away by you was witched
the shaggy hide I hunted—
and sheltered here?
So meet a mate
it were hard from such merry
maidens to hold.

(*The maidens laugh aloud.*)

WOGLINDE.

Siegfried, say what thou'lt give,
if back the game we bring thee?

SIEGFRIED.

Yet bide I bootyless;
so seek what seems to you best.

WELLGUNDE.

A golden ring
girdles thy finger.—

THE THREE MAIDENS
(together).

That give us!

SIEGFRIED.

With a whelming Worm
I wrestled for it once;
shall I barter it now to buy
the paws of a paltry bear?

WOGLINDE.

Such is thy greed?

WELLGUNDE.

So seek'st thou for gain?

FLOSSHILDE.

Free givers
fits it women should find.

SIEGFRIED.

To spend in such sport my goods
would help me to grief at home.

FLOSSHILDE.

Is thy wife so hard?

WELLGUNDE.

So fierce of hand?

WOGLINDE.

He already feels its fall.
(They laugh.)

SIEGFRIED.
Now laugh and make your mirth!
Not long I mean it to last;
the hoop your hearts so need,
you Nodders never shall have.

FLOSSHILDE.
So sweet!

WELLGUNDE.
So strong!

WOGLINDE.
So worth a wish!

THE THREE
(together).
How sad his greed should seem so great!
(*They laugh and dive below.*)

SIEGFRIED
(*coming further down the slope*).
What makes me bear
their truthless blame,
and take their slander so?—
Rise they again
to the river's rim,
the ring they want shall await them.—
Here, here, you wayward
water-women,
in haste! the ring you shall have.

THE THREE RHINE-DAUGHTERS
(*come up again, and show themselves earnest and solemn*).
Withhold it, hero,
and ward it well,
until thou hast read the hurt
thou harbour'st in the ring.
Glad feel if we come
to free thee then of its curse.

SIEGFRIED
(quietly putting the ring again on his finger).
Now sing what you foresee!

THE RHINE-DAUGHTERS
(separately and together).
Siegfried! Siegfried! Siegfried!
Harm for thee we behold.
 To raise thee sorrow
 sav'st thou the ring!
 From the Rhine was gathered
 unwrought its gold;
he, who guilefully shaped it
 and lost it with shame,
called on it a dark
 undying curse,
 that hastens to death
 him whom it decks.
 As the Worm thou slewest,
 wilt thou be slain,
 and here to-day
 —be deep in thy heed—
wilt thou not sell us the ring,
for the Rhine to sink in its water.
 The flood alone
 its curse can allay.

SIEGFRIED.
 You crafty women,
 waste not words!
Caught me little your kindness,
of your threats still less I am thoughtful.

THE RHINE-DAUGHTERS.
 Siegfried! Siegfried!
 No falsehood we say;
fly the curse that was kindled!
 At night by working
 Norns it was woven
 in the endless coil
 of counsel of old.

SIEGFRIED.

My sword once splintered a spear;—
    the endless coil
    of counsel of old,
    wove they with wasting
    curses its web,
Norns shall not cover from Nothung!
    Once warned me beware
    of the curse a Worm;
but he failed to wake me to fear,—
    the world's riches
    I won with a ring,
    that for love's delight
    swiftly I'd leave;
I'll yield it for sweetness to you;
but for safety of limbs and of life,—
    were not its worth
    of a finger's weight,—
no ring from me you will reach!
    For limbs and their life
    —left without love
    to be fast bound
    by fear with its fetters—
    limbs and their life—
    look!—so
forth from me far I send!

(*He has picked up a clod of earth from the ground, and, with the last words, has thrown it over his head behind him.*)

THE RHINE-DAUGHTERS.

    Fly, sisters!
    Fast from his folly!
    As strong and wise
    himself he weens,
as he burdened and blinded is seen.
    Oaths he swore—
    and he answers them not;
    runes he knows—
    and he reads them not;

a godly good
he had for gift—
how he has slighted it
sees he not;
of the ring, that will deal him death,
alone he is loath to be rid !—

Farewell, Siegfried !
A dauntless woman
to-day as thy heir will be greeted;
she gives us easier ear.
To her ! To her ! To her !

(They swim, singing, away.)

SIEGFRIED
(looks after them with a smile).
On land, I learn, and on water
like are women in ways;
whom flattery fails to thaw,
with threats they think to fright him;
who scorns their scaring face,
he fleetly will find they scold.—
And yet—
yoked me not Gutrun' fast,
the gladdest and fairest swimmer
sweetly had felt my sway !

(The cries of hunting-horns approach from the height; Siegfried answers merrily on his horn.)

(Gunther, Hagen and men come, during what follows, down from the height.)

HAGEN
(yet on the height).
Hoyho !

SIEGFRIED.
Hoyho !

THE MEN.
Hoyho ! Hoyho !

HAGEN.
Find we at last
how far thou hast fled?

SIEGFRIED.
Come below! fresh and cool it feels.

HAGEN.
So meet for rest,
and right for the meal.
Unload the booty,
and broach the leathers!

(*The game is laid in a heap; drink-horns and wine-skins are brought. All then lie down.*)

HAGEN.
His speed has harmed our sport;
so shall you hear of wonders
that Siegfried's hunt has worked.

SIEGFRIED
(*laughing*).
Ill fare I for food;
at others' booty
I beg to bite.

HAGEN.
Thou bootyless?

SIEGFRIED.
I hied for wood-sport out,
but water-game only beheld;
had I counted on such comers,
three wayward water-fowl
I fairly had brought to booty,
who sang, as they sat before me,
I here to-day should be slain.

(*Gunther starts, and looks darkly at Hagen.*)

HAGEN.
Such were a spiteful sport,
where the hapless hunter himself
an unthankful beast should slaughter!

SIEGFRIED.

I'm thirsty!

(*He has placed himself between Hagen and Gunther; full drink-horns are handed to them.*)

HAGEN.

I've heard it whispered, Siegfried,—
what say the birds in singing
thou rightly can'st tell;—
were such the truth?

SIEGFRIED.

For long I've minded
their lisping no more.

(*He drinks and then hands his horn to Gunther.*)

Drink, Gunther, drink!
Thy brother bids begin.

GUNTHER
(*gazing thoughtfully and gloomily into the horn*).

It looks but poor and pale;—
thy blood alone thou bring'st!

SIEGFRIED
(*laughing*).

With bloom of thine I blend it!

(*He pours from Gunther's horn into his own till it overflows.*)

To leap the lip they mingle;
on mother earth
fall it with freshening ease!

GUNTHER
(*sighing*).

What makes so high thy mirth?

SIEGFRIED
(*lightly to Hagen*).

He finds Brünnhild' his match?

HAGEN.

Might he but fathom her,
as thou the birds thou hear'st!

SIEGFRIED.

Since women I made my singers,
has slept my mood for the woods.

HAGEN.

They sent thee once their song!

SIEGFRIED.

Come! Gunther!
Comfortless man!
Freely for thanks,
with tales I'll befriend thee
about my times of boyhood.

GUNTHER.

I'll gladly hear.

HAGEN.

So, hero, sing!

(*All place themselves close about Siegfried, who alone sits upright, while the others stretch themselves further on the ground.*)

SIEGFRIED.

Mime was named
a muttering dwarf,
who with endless grudge
guided me up,
in hope the boy,
when bigger and bold,
in the wood should slay him the Worm,
who slept on a hidden hoard.
In smoke I was held,
to hammer and smelt;
till where the smith
was weak at his work,
the learner's mettle
made him a master—
so that a broken blade he welded
sound from its worthless bits.
My father's sword
freshly I set;

   never than now
   firmer was Nothung;
   fit for the deed
   deemed it the dwarf;
so forth to the wood we went;
and I felled him Fafner, the Worm.—

   Now for your whole
   heed is the news;
wonders wait for your knowledge.
   With his blood I felt
   my fingers on fire;
I laid them fast to my lips;
   and hardly had tasted
   the heat on my tongue,—
when, what a bird above me
now sang—in words I saw.
The boughs he sat as he said;—
   "Hi! Siegfried shall have now
   the Nibelungs' hoard,
   for here in the hole
   it awaits his hand!
Let him not turn from the tarn-helm,
it leads him to tasks of delight;
but finds he a ring for his finger,
the world he will rule with his will!"

    HAGEN.
Ring and tarn-helm
found'st thou in truth?

    THE MEN.
And talked thy friend to thee further?

    SIEGFRIED.
   Ring and helm
   rightly I held;
   to lisp again
   he began as I listened,—
and sat aloft while he sang;—

"Hi! Siegfried is holder
of ring now and helm;
but trust in Mime
no more he may try!
The hoard at his hand he but looked for;
now lies he in wait by the way;
for the life of Siegfried he searches;
let Mime with Siegfried not meddle!"

HAGEN.
And wise were his words?

THE MEN.
Was Mime outwitted?

SIEGFRIED.
With drink for my death
he near to me drew;
told with tottering
tongue of his falseness;
Nothung finished his talk.

HAGEN
(*laughing*).
The sword he had failed at
found he so friendly?

THE MEN.
What bade the bird to thee further?

HAGEN
(*after squeezing the juice of a herb into the drink-horn*).
Hero, drink;
for here my horn
shall deal thee a draught I mixed,
that thy thought might not be faithless
to things that are far and folded!

SIEGFRIED
(*after he has drunk*).
In sorrow aloft
I sought through the leaves,
where still he stayed and sang;—

"Hi! Siegfried the slippery
dwarf has slain!
Now, would he might win
the lordliest wife!
Afar she sleeps on a height,
a fire besets her hall;
he baffles the blaze,
he wakens the bride,
Brünnhild' he wins to his breast!"
(*Gunther listens with growing wonder.*)

HAGEN.
And had the bird's
behest thy heed?

SIEGFRIED.
Soon as he said it
forward I set,
till the fiery rock I reached;
I parted the flame,
and found for pay—
sweetly a woman asleep
in midst of her warding mail.
Her head I helped
from clasp of the helm;
my kiss awakened her wide;—
ah, like a fire I felt
on my body Brünnhilde's arms!

GUNTHER.
How says he?
(*Two ravens rise from a thicket, wheel over Siegfried, and fly away.*)

HAGEN.
And ravens' riddles
as well can'st thou read?
(*Siegfried starts sharply up and, turning his back towards Hagen, looks after the ravens.*)

HAGEN.
Murder rouse they in me!
(*He thrusts his spear into Siegfried's back; Gunther—too late—seizes his arm.*)

GUNTHER AND THE MEN.
Hagen! what mean'st thou?

(*Siegfried with both hands swings up his shield, to crush Hagen with it; his strength leaves him; the shield sinks from his hand; he himself with a crash falls over it.*)

HAGEN
(*pointing to him as he lies on the ground*).
His oath is on him!

(*He turns quietly aside, and walks slowly away over the height, till he disappears.*)
(*Gunther in grief bends down to Siegfried's side. The men stand sadly round him as he dies. Long silence of the deepest distress. At the coming of the ravens twilight had already begun to fall.*)

SIEGFRIED
(*with a flash once more opening his eyes, and beginning with solemn voice*).

  Brünnhilde—
   holiest bride—
 behold! lift up thy lashes!—
   Why again
  to sleep art thou gone?
Who drowns thee in slumber so deep?
    The wakener came;
   with kiss he calls;
  he breaks from the bride
  the fetters that bound her;
till Brünnhild' laughs for delight!—
    Ah!—for her eyes
   are open for ever!—
    Ah!—for her breath
   is billows of blessing!—
   Swallowing sweetness—
    happiest horror;—
  greeting Brünnhilde bids!—

(*He dies.*)
(*The men lift the body on to the shield and carry it in solemn train slowly away over the height. Gunther walks nearest the body. The moon breaks out through clouds, and lights the mournful procession along the height. Then from the Rhine mists rise, and gradually fill the whole stage up to the front. When the mist parts again the scene is changed.*)

The Gibichungs' Hall. (With the space by the river, as in the first act. Night. Moonlight is reflected in the Rhine. Gutrune comes out of her chamber into the hall.)

GUTRUNE.
Heard I his horn?
(She listens.)
Hark!—Not
yet is he near.—
Sickening dreams
have daunted me in sleep!—
Wildly heard I
whinny his horse;—
Brünnhild's laughter
awoke me at last.—
Who was the woman
that went to-wards the Rhine?—
How Brünnhild' haunts me!—
Bides she at home?
(She listens at a door on the right, and then calls softly.)
Brünnhild'! Brünnhild'!—
Art thou up?—
(She timidly opens the door and looks in.)
Bare is her bed!—
So she it was,
that I watched to-wards the Rhine?—
(She becomes frightened and listens towards the distance.)
He is it now?—
No!—
None is hither.—
Siegfried only be soon!

(She is about to turn again to her chamber; as she, however, hears Hagen's voice, she stops, and, fixed with fear, stands for some time without moving.)

HAGEN'S
(voice from without, coming nearer).
Hoyho! Hoyho!
Awake! Awake!
Torches! Torches!
Forth with fire!

Home comes
the quarry from hunt.
Hoyho! Hoyho!

(*Light and growing flash of fire from without.*)

HAGEN
(*coming into the hall*).
Wake, Gutrun',
and welcome Siegfried!
The hero nears
by now his home.

(*Men and Women, with lights and firebrands, accompany in great confusion the train of those who are coming home with Siegfried's body, among whom is Gunther.*)

GUTRUNE
(*in great dread*)
What befell, Hagen?
I heard not his horn!

HAGEN.
His mouth is pale,
it blows no more;
he goes not to forest
or fight again;
nor woos for the winsomest women!

GUTRUNE
(*with growing terror*).
What bring the men?

HAGEN.
From a murd'ring boar his booty;
Siegfried, who by him was slain!

(*Gutrune screams and throws herself on the body, which has been set down in the middle of the hall. General emotion and sorrow.*)

GUNTHER
(*as he tries to lift the fainting Gutrune*).
Gutrune, sweetest sister!
Waken thy sight!
Say me a word!

GUTRUNE
(coming to herself).
Siegfried!—Siegfried is slain!
She thrusts Gunther impetuously back.)
Hence, treacherous brother!
Thy hand has killed my husband!
    O help! Help!
    Sorrow! Sorrow!
Among them Siegfried they murdered!

GUNTHER.
Who sets on me the harm?
For Hagen save thy summons;
no other the cursed boar is,
who killed this matchless man.

HAGEN.
Have I for such thy hate?

GUNTHER.
    Ill and sorrow
    seize thee for ever!

HAGEN
(coming close, with terrible defiance).
Yea then! His death is my doing;
    I—Hagen—
    hit to his heart!
His life he owed to my spear,
that sped his lying oath.
Meetly I've wrought, and made
boundless my right of booty;
which so I seize in this ring.

GUNTHER.
Away!—What now is mine
thy meed thou never shalt make.

HAGEN.
Be round me, men, in my right!

GUNTHER.
Shamelessly seizes Gutrun's
heirdom the Niblung's son?

HAGEN
(*drawing his sword*).
The Niblung's heirdom
reaches so—his son !

(*He attacks Gunther; he defends himself; they fight. The men throw themselves between them. Gunther, at a stroke of Hagen's, falls dead to the ground.*)

HAGEN.
Here—the ring !

(*He grasps at Siegfried's hand, which lifts itself threateningly up. General horror. Gutrune and the women scream aloud. From the background Brünnhilde strides firmly and solemnly towards the front.*)

BRÜNNHILDE
(*still in the background*).
Swerve from the whelming
sound of your woe !
On the way of her vengeance
treads the wife you betrayed.
(*She steps calmly further forwards.*)
Babes I meet,
who whimper for their mother,
when wholesome milk they have wasted,
but leave such lordly
sorrow unlifted
as beseems the man that you mourn.

GUTRUNE.
Brünnhild', the grudge that grieved thee
has brought on our heads this harm !
To heat the men to his murder
woe that we welcomed thee here !

BRÜNNHILDE.
Poor woman, peace !
His wife thou hast barely been ;
as harlot alone
had'st thou his heart.

The wife that he wed am I ;
he had sworn to me endless oaths,
ere sight of thy face he found.

GUTRUNE
(in wildest despair).
O hateful Hagen !
Woe ! Ah, woe !
That with the drink he helped me
to wile her husband from her !
O Sorrow ! Sorrow !
How swiftly I deem
that Brünnhild's indeed the bride
I gave him drink to forget !

(Full of shame she turns away from Siegfried, and with grief bends over Gunther's body; she remains thus—motionless—till the end. Long silence. Hagen, sunk in gloomy thought and leaning on his spear and shield, stands defiantly at the extremity of the other side.)

BRÜNNHILDE
(alone in the middle; after she has for a long while, at first with a deep shudder, then with almost overpowering sadness, contemplated Siegfried's face, she turns with solemn exaltation to the men and women).
Build me with logs
aloft on his brim
a heap for the Rhine to heed ;
fast and far
tower the flame,
as it licks the limbs
the highest hero has left !—
His horse guide to my hand,
to be gone with me to his master ;
for amidst his holiest
meed to be with him
I long in every limb.—
Fulfil Brünnhilde's bent !

(The younger men, during what follows, raise a great funeral pile in front of the hall, near the bank of the Rhine; women dress it with hangings, on which they strew herbs and flowers.)

BRÜNNHILDE
(again lost in contemplation of Siegfried's body).
Like a look of sun
he sends me his light ;

Dusk of the Gods.

    his soul was faultless
    that false I found !
    His bride he betrayed
    by truth to his brother,
    and from her whose haunt
    was wholly his bosom,
barred himself with his sword.—
    Sounder than his,
    are oaths not sworn with ;
    better than his,
held never are bargains ;
    holier than his,
    love is unheard of ;
    and yet to all oaths,
    to every bargain,
    to faithfullest love too—
has lied never his like !—

See you how it was so ?—

    O you, who heed
    our oaths in your heaven,
    open your eyes
    on the bloom of my ill—
and watch your unwithering blame !
    For my summons hark,
    thou highest god !
Him, by his daringest deed—
that filled so fitly thy hope,
    darkly thy means
    doomed in its midst
to ruin's merciless wrong ;
    me—too
    to betray he was bounden,
that wise a woman might be !

Guess I not now of thy good ?—

    Nothing ! Nothing !
    Nought is hidden ;
all is owned to me here !

Fitly thy ravens
take to their feathers;
with tidings dreadly dreamed for,
hence to their home they shall go.
Slumber! Slumber, thou god!—

(*She signs to the men to lift Siegfried's body and bear it to the funeral pile; at the same time she draws the ring from Siegfried's finger, contemplates it during what follows, and at last puts it on her own.*)

My heirdom here
behold me hallow!—

Thou guilty ring!
Ruining gold!
My hand gathers,
and gives thee again.
You wisely-seeing
water-sisters,
the Rhine's unresting daughters,
I deem your word was of weight!
All that you ask
now is your own;
here from my ashes'
heap you may have it!—
The flame as it clasps me round,
free from its curse the ring!—
Back to its gold
unbind it again,
and far in the flood
withhold its fire,
the Rhine's unslumbering sun,
that for harm from him was reft.—

(*She turns towards the back, where Siegfried's body lies already on the pile, and seizes from a man the great firebrand.*)

Away, you ravens!
Whisper to your master
what here among us you heard!
By Brünnhild's rock
your road shall be bent;
who roars yet round it,
Loge—warn him to Walhall!

For with doom of gods
is darkened the day;
so—set I the torch
to Walhall's towering walls.

(*She flings the brand into the heap of wood, which quickly blazes up. Two ravens have flown up from the bank, and disappear towards the background.*)*

Two young men bring in the horse; Brünnhilde seizes and quickly unbridles it.)

Grane, my horse,
hail to thee here!
Knowest thou, friend,
how far I shall need thee?

---

* *Before the poem was put to music the following additional lines were at this place given to Brünnhilde, as she once more turned to the bystanders:—*

You, blossoming life's
abiding abode,
of my words be mindful,
mark what they mean!
See you in fathomless fire
Siegfried and Brünnhilde fade,—
see you the River's daughters
go down to the deep with the ring,—
to northward now
look through the night;
afar if heaven
is holy with fire,
be held by all
that Walhall's end you behold!—

When once the gods
like wind are gone,
when without wielders
I've left the world,
to my holiest wisdom's hoard
I help it here on its way.—
Not goods, nor gold,
nor greatness of gods;
not house, nor land,
nor lordly life;

Behold how lightens
hither thy lord,
Siegfried —my sorrowless hero.
To go to him now
neigh'st thou so gladly?
Lure thee to him
the light and the laughter?—
Feel how my bosom
fills with its blaze!
Hands of fire
hold me at heart;
fully to fold him,
to feel I am felt,
in masterless love
to be laid to his limbs!—

---

not burdensome bargains'
treacherous bands,
not wont with the lying
weight of its law;
happy, in luck or need,
holds you nothing but love.—

As the poet in these lines had already endeavoured, with sententious thought, to supply in anticipation the musical working of the drama,—so in the course of the long interruptions which kept him from the musical completion of his poem, he felt himself moved to the following conception of the last parting lines, as more calculated to produce such working:—

Fare I now no more
to Walhall's fastness,
where is the rest I ride to?
From Wish-home forth are my feet
Dream-home walk they no further;
the gaping gates
of boundless being
here behind me I bar;
to the will-less holy
home of my hunger,
the world-wanderer's goal,
for birth not again to bind me,
guarded in knowledge I go.

Heiaho! Grane!
Greeting to him!
Siegfried! Brünnhild' see!
Happy hails thee thy bride!

(*She has swung herself stormily on to the horse, and rides it with a leap into the burning pile. The flame at once soars crackling on high, so that the fire fills the whole space in front of the hall, and seems almost to seize on the hall itself. In terror the women press to the foreground. Suddenly the fire sinks, so that nothing but a gloomy heat-cloud remains hanging over the place; this rises and completely parts; the Rhine has violently swollen forward from its bank, and rolls its water over the place of the fire, up to the threshold of the hall. The Three Rhine-Daughters have swum forward on its waves. —Hagen, who since what happened with the ring has in growing anxiety watched Brünnhilde's demeanour, at the sight of the Rhine-Daughters is seized with the greatest dread; he hurriedly flings away spear, shield, and helmet, and with the cry, "Unhand the ring!" plunges, as if out of his senses, into the flood. Woglinde and Wellgunde wind his neck in their arms, and so draw him with them as they swim back into the deep; Flosshilde, in front of the others, holds exultingly on high the ring which she has seized.—In the sky, at the same time, breaks out from the distance a reddish glow like the Northern Light, which grows continually broader and stronger. —The men and women, in speechless commotion, watch both the action and the appearance in the sky.—The curtain falls.*)

Happy ease
from all that's endless,—
ween you how it was won?
Suffering love's
most sunken sorrow
widely opened my eyes;
wither saw I the world.—

In the end it could not but be evident to the composer that these lines, their thought being already expressed with the greatest clearness in the working of the drama as given with its music, could not in actual representation be retained.

ERRATUM.

Page 77, top; after WOTAN insert
(*deep in contemplation of the castle*).

TO RICHARD WAGNER

WITH A PRIVATELY PRINTED COPY OF
"DUSK OF THE GODS."

("*So musst du ihn lieben.*")

To hope was hard when first I heard it said,
from bird to bud in fitful fields of Spring,
that I, whose ease was love for everything
that made itself my own in heart or head
by dint of beauty, lo had found instead
a labour left undone for me to do ;—
and here again were grief, when further two
of life's unlasting years are harvested
and sounds of seated Summer in the land
beset me like a solace while above
an ended work I lift the farewell hand,
but that the time has taught me :—if it prove
that love in less than love could understand
an answer, it were less itself than love.

Summer, 1875.

"THE NIBELUNG'S RING."

Mr. Alfred Forman's Translation of "Der Ring des Nibelungen."

Richard Wagner :—
  .... Für diesen Eifer und diese Liebe sage ich Ihnen meinen wärmsten Dank, und soll es mich sehr freuen wenn Sie diese schöne Arbeit dem Wagner-Verein und ins besondere meinem Freund Herrn Dannreuther übergeben.

Algernon Charles Swinburne :—
  I do not wonder at the cordiality of commendation bestowed by the master on such a version of his great work.

Hans von Bülow :—
  A most marvellous translation.

John Payne :—
  Mr. Alfred Forman has successfully accomplished a task which might rebut the boldest of translators.

Richard Garnett :—
  Mr. Forman's translation is a marvellous *tour de force*.

Edward Dannreuther :—
  Forman's translation was a labour of love. He never departs from the form or spirit of the original.

Athenæum :—
  Intending visitors to the performances of Wagner's colossal work cannot be too strongly urged to peruse Mr. Alfred Forman's admirable translation of the poem.

Academy :—
  The extraordinary difficulty of the task may be imagined when it is said that not merely is the English version fitted to the music, the rhythm and metre being closely adhered to, but that even the alliterative verse has been preserved in the translation.

Standard :—

The spirit of the poem can best be seized through Mr. Forman's really admirable translation.

Daily News :—

A very close translation.

Morning Post :—

Mr. Forman has been deservedly praised by Wagner and Von Bülow for the excellence of his work.

Daily Chronicle :—

In Mr. Forman's work we are borne into an ideal sphere. We wonder at the wealth of pregnant words; we are entranced by the unity of style and feeling; and under his guidance we traverse the new world of poetry which Wagner himself has revealed to us.

Globe :—

Mr. Forman's version supplies a public want. It has the merit of following the original very closely, both in meaning and form.

St. James's Gazette :—

Mr. Forman has produced what must in itself be regarded as a fine poem.

Evening News :—

Mr. Alfred Forman's admirable translation of the gigantic tetralogy "Der Ring des Nibelungen," is entitled to rank as a valuable contribution to the dramatic literature of the day.

Court Circular :—

Wagner is to be greatly congratulated on having found an interpreter who has recognized in "Der Ring des Nibelungen" a tragic poem of the first importance, and who has rendered it into English in such a manner as to convey the same impression.

Weekly Dispatch :—

A splendid translation. . . Mr. Forman's task has evidently been a labour of love.

Weekly Times :—

The diction of Mr. Forman's translation is everywhere marked by that inventive and organizing sense of language which is the gift of only a born poet.

London Figaro :—

An admirable English adaptation. . . . This was the version approved by Wagner.

Society :—

In Mr. Alfred Forman's translation, the alliterative beauty and Teutonic strength of the original have been preserved in a manner that is simply marvellous.

Musical Standard :—

The philological import of Mr. Forman's work is as great as its poetic charm. We rise from perusal of the transcription with the consciousness that we have passed through the same world and received the same impressions as during our reading of the original.

Musical World :—

A masterly version, or rather marvellous counterpart of the original.

Musical Times :—

None but a genuine enthusiast would have dreamed of undertaking so herculean a work as this translation. . . . It can be honestly recommended as giving an excellent idea both of the spirit and form of the work.

Manchester Examiner :—

Mr. Alfred Forman's version is at once a poem in itself, and one in which the spirit of the original is faithfully reproduced.

Northern Echo :—

To have failed in such an undertaking would have been to have excited admiration for the boldness of the attempt. To have succeeded is a felicity any Englishman of letters might envy.

Vienna Neues Fremden-Blatt :—

The existence of so valuable a translation as Forman's should serve to spread continually wider and wider the interest in and the understanding of Wagner's creations in England.

Glasenapp's " Life of Wagner " :—

The translation of the poem of " Der Ring des Nibelungen," by Alfred Forman, has the reputation of being a work of monumental importance.

BY THE SAME AUTHOR.

TRISTAN AND ISOLDE

English words to Richard Wagner's "Tristan und Isolde" in the mixed Alliterative and Rhyming metres of the original.

The only English Version approved by Wagner.

Musical World :—
    Mr. Forman has endowed our literature with a work that will stand alone in that department which bears the heading "Richard Wagner," for we feel justified in ranking it even higher than this gentleman's own version of the "Ring."

In Preparation.

PARSIFAL

English words to Richard Wagner's Consecration-Festival-Play.

Lightning Source UK Ltd.
Milton Keynes UK
UKHW010639280223
417789UK00004B/203